Advance Praise for *Edit Your Life*

"Living intentionally in our messy world requires work. Fortunately, in this inspiring and practical guide, Elisabeth shows us how to edit out what doesn't matter—so we have more time for what does."

—Laura Vanderkam, author of *Tranquility by Tuesday*

"*Edit Your Life* is a practical and philosophical guide to editing as a life practice, and a bighearted call to live a happier, more deliberate life."

—Kim Cross, author of *What Stands in a Storm*

"A book of distilled wisdom and a life-transforming guide inviting readers to personalize what an 'edited' life means to them and what they need to let go."

—Elizabeth Filippouli, editor of *From Women to the World: Letters for a New Century*

Praise for Previous Works by Elisabeth Sharp McKetta

"Elisabeth McKetta is a wonderful storyteller who takes us generously into her life, which always seems initially off-balance, full of falls, disappointments, and reversals, and yet, in the end, joyous."

—Phillip Lopate, author of *To Show and to Tell: The Craft of Literary Nonfiction*

"Captivating and evocative and original."

—Grace Dane Mazur, author of *The Garden Party*

"Elisabeth Sharp McKetta examines the work of becoming oneself through the battle between the longing for travel and the desire for home."

—Kyoko Mori, author of *The Dream of Water* and *Shizuko's Daughter*

"For some years now, I have been reading and appreciating Elisabeth Sharp McKetta's exceptional Poetry for Strangers project. With generosity, inclusiveness, and openness to the wonders of nature and the human spirit, McKetta reaches out to those strangers, encountered by chance, inviting them to participate in an art form that non-writers so often consider alien territory. She is a bridge-builder of the most original kind."

—Lydia Davis, author of *Can't and Won't* and *Essays One*

Edit Your Life

Edit Your Life

A HANDBOOK FOR LIVING WITH
INTENTION IN A MESSY WORLD

Elisabeth Sharp McKetta

A TarcherPerigee Book

tarcherperigee

an imprint of Penguin Random House LLC
penguinrandomhouse.com

Most TarcherPerigee books are available at special quantity discounts for bulk purchase for sales promotions, premiums, fund-raising, and educational needs. Special books or book excerpts also can be created to fit specific needs. For details, write: SpecialMarkets@penguinrandomhouse.com.

Hardcover ISBN 9780593539385
Ebook ISBN 9780593539392

Printed in the United States of America
1st Printing

Book design by Shannon Nicole Plunkett

*For anyone who wishes to live a more deliberate life
and isn't sure where to start: this book is for you.*

*And for my wise, wacky, much-loved children,
who chose their own pseudonyms.*

And always for James.

CONTENTS

Welcome

Thank you for coming to this book. I wish for it to serve as a sort of organizing book for the soul, offering ideas—both practical and philosophical—to distill any life to its ideal shape. I have tried to write it in the same way that I would speak with a friend as we sit together on the deck, watching the evening close around us, drinking wine or tea, talking late into the night about our lives.

Editing is an act of change; it requires asking "What is this now?" and "What should it be?" Editing means assessing the form something wants to take and cutting out what is unnecessary. Whether a book or a relationship, a kitchen or a parenting philosophy, the principles are the same. In this book I will use the term *life-edit*, which means exactly that. This book is not about home editing (though the same principles apply to curating a stance on life as to curating objects in a house), nor is it about literary editing, though I will draw upon my editing experience to share its most life-applicable skills.

Editing is a skill that helps us see anything clearly—to look, and look again. This book is about skills that transcend the specifics of our lives: Whether you have a partner or not, dependents or not, a job or a career or a calling, wherever you live and whatever you earn, you can use the principles of life-editing to rethink how you spend your hours, days, and years. I will share my own experience, and I hope you will use it to reflect upon your own experience. The details of your life are as specific to you as mine are to me—and below those details, we are all trying to live a life that is worthy of us.

> Editing is a skill that helps us see anything clearly.

Often life gets edited for us. This is unavoidable: We cannot control the world outside our homes. In many cases, we cannot control the world *inside* our homes. Even if we do not court change, life is full of it: we must respond both to changes that involve gain, such as falling in love, finding a new job, starting school, having a baby, moving to a new place—and to changes that involve loss, whether of a loved one, of a job, of a home, of one's health, or (hello, pandemic!) all of the above. Any crisis forces us to realign, let alone an unprecedented worldwide one. When we lose things that have felt certain and necessary, life gets edited for us against our will, and we are forced, often at an inconvenient time, to reevaluate.

While defensive editing—editing in response to changes—is something we all must do at times, this book proposes *proactive life-editing*: not waiting for "the right time" but editing now, in whatever situation, as a way to take an active role in shaping our lives around what matters most. In this way, we can make decisions as clearly as possible about what our life needs and wants to be. We can—with a little thought, an open mind, and a willingness to try a few simple changes—edit our needs to their essentials, revisit and reprioritize our values, then figure out how best to go on. We have all been forced to edit and will be forced to again, and my hope is that this book takes that unavoidable fact and turns it into a quest that anyone can do with a sense of clarity, grit, self-respect, resourcefulness, and even joy.

When is the best time to edit? Most people edit when crisis comes or life changes—when the relationship fails, the money grows too tight to ignore, the unhappy work environment leads to health problems or emotional burnout, or the children are grown, or some other intervention requires us to change our stance. A wiser way to edit is in advance of that, anytime your life feels out of alignment. You can always edit your way back, or partway back, as needed—a great number of decisions in life can be revised or reversed.

The risk of waiting comes with the risk of regret: by failing to edit when our life doesn't quite fit, we miss giving the best of our attention to our lives—wishing our lives away, wishing they were different. The risk of waiting comes too with the risk of disengagement: a sense that all our life's parts, including its people, have been reduced to items on an endless list. This leads to a feeling of everyday claustrophobia, a grief and guilt at having abandoned the essential things.

This is why wherever you are, whenever you are reading this, if you have picked up this book with a question in your mind about your life and how it might be better, the time to edit is now.

When you edit proactively, you are not making yourself crisis-proof—that is not possible—but you are raising the likelihood that future crises will not stem from your choices and habits, and that when life forces you to tilt, you can tilt back with relative ease. Editing paves a way for you to connect deeply with yourself and the choices you have made. Editing ensures self-trust: that you will not regret the part you played in your own life.

Most people are better teachers of things we learned with effort than things that came naturally to us. I wrote this book because I struggle with this stuff. I've designed my life around these principles, yet never for a single day have I upheld them perfectly. Still, I am better for the trying.

Any writer knows that good writing comes not from good first drafts, but from good editing. As a professional editor and teacher of writing, I spend thousands of hours every year talking with writers about how to edit their work into the best forms possible. These conversations, not always but often, take a more personal turn: into the writer's life. Is the life they are living supporting the work they are striving to do? The ideas and skills of editing—look closely, identify first choices, ask if it is necessary, and more—are applicable to every single part of our lives. The skills of editing have become my habit and my instinct. So when my family was stuck in a living situation that felt unsustainable, the clearest way forward was for me to ask myself how I might edit my way out of it.

Several years ago, my family—husband James, six-year-old daughter Cora, three-year-old son Scott, two Labradors (one old—who died early in this venture—and one young), and I—made the choice to move into our 275-square-foot backyard guesthouse in Boise, Idaho. We spent six months discussing it as a family, concocting a plan that met everybody's needs and a few of our first-choice wants (the children's first-choice wants were to keep their favorite toys and to still have sleepovers—check and check). And then we moved.

We call where we live "The Shed." It has an aqua concrete floor, a kitchenette, a bathroom, an expandable dining table that folds into a desk, and a ladder up a two-story bookshelf that leads to a sleeping loft. The kids have their own bedroom with a Murphy bunk bed. The Shed is roughly one-tenth the size of the average American house and it requires us to spend a lot of time in close proximity. It is also very beautiful, in a simple, practical, clean way. There is room for everything we need and love—but nothing more.

We moved here because we needed a big edit. Once upon a time, we lived in a big house that we hoped would serve as a container for all the lives we wished to live. The five lives that matter most to me are mother, writer, teacher, spouse, friend. My spouse has his own set of lives, and my children are figuring out theirs. For a time, though, a single life dominated us: home dweller. My husband and I found ourselves, five years into parenthood, feeling far from the people we wished to be. Our good intentions for our lives felt lost in the clutter of our obligations, all of which felt centered around various forms of housekeeping: tidying, thinking about, cleaning, organizing, and paying for the house. We had moved into the house hoping it would provide a safe backdrop for our lives, which it did—but gradually, its responsibilities had seeped into the foreground and become our major activities. On any given day, it seemed I spent more time on home management than I spent writing, teaching, talking with my husband and my friends, or playing with my children: the parts of my life that mattered most.

We were in crisis, though we did not know to what extent. Every day we were faced with the facts of how easily the big ship that was our life could be sunk. Sunk in our distractedness; sunk financially; sunk in yesterday's work; sunk in our habits; sunk in a state of constant mess; sunk in our souls. My greatest exhaustion came when I crossed the threshold from the outside world to the house: for *there was just so much to do.* At home, I was always multitasking and half listening. My default mode had become distraction.

We needed to free up vital energy, to edit something out, or we would miss all these years, remembering only the chaos and none of the beauty. The life-edit that made the most sense to us was a radical change: to move into a house so small that the local elementary school brought its first graders there on a field trip to see how small a house can be (they had to come in two shifts so that everybody could fit). Life changes need not be so radical, of course, to accomplish the same goal. We made a big life-edit, though subtler edits can be just as effective. From facing that edit that I had feared so much, I learned the great value of lightening one's life, and how it enables one to face it, unafraid.

For with life-editing comes a lesson, different for everyone. In addition to all the traceable and physical things you shed, you shed some old emotional baggage that has held you back. For me it was an unconscious feeling of disempowerment, a waiting to be rescued. Like magic, it vanished when we edited out other people's expectations for what life at home should look like. I learned, in our leap, to self-rescue: that I am capable of—and even good at—solving problems creatively and collaboratively when in a pinch. In claiming this knowledge, I shed the invisible assumption that someone else could or should solve the ordinary problems of my life. I hadn't realized I was carrying around that assumption. How did it get there? What was it doing squatting in my mind, uninvited? Yet in moving to the Shed, suddenly I recognized that much of the lightness I felt was the absence of that old fear.

Furthermore, life-editing taught me trust at a new and deeper level: For the first time as an adult, I could trust that there would be enough—enough time, money, energy—so that I didn't have to spend my life worried and in scarcity mode. This confidence grew slowly, as we learned as a family to need less and to enjoy what we had more; to do fewer activities, each with better focus; to spend less on day-to-day needs; and to lay away more for what may come. To rent out the house and live comfortably behind it, treating life at home—for this sweet and complicated era, however long it lasted—as a great adventure. It was a single edit. Yet the ripples of this edit were immense. The children learned to share all things, to tidy as they go, to choose creative projects that could be done in any space, and to become the sort of travelers who feel at home in the world. My husband and I suddenly had time for each other—lots of it. For the first time, I felt fully emancipated. I had learned something new about what I was made of. What we all were made of.

By practicing these principles, you will shed something too: some long-held feeling that gets mightily in the way. In short, life-editing helps raise our emotional ceilings and refresh our assumptions about ourselves.

An edited life is personal to you. It can be any size and shape that allows you to live deliberately and with what you love at the center. It has little to do with what you have and more to do with how you feel. Editing for one person may be centered around music, or food, or the ocean. Or books, or travel, or school, or friends, or a garden, or children. The edited life is an alignment between what you love and what fills your day. It is that simple. This process excavates the ideal life and asks how it can be made as real as possible.

Editing begets editing. Learning to see what is possible and actualizing it is one of the world's most portable skills. Editing one area of life teaches us, inevitably, how to do it in another. Editing your morning routine or when you check email will inevitably clear a pathway for change in other more important areas: how you work, love, and play. Making any kind of life-edit teaches us a great deal about what we need, on a soul level, in order to flourish. We need less than we think in some ways, more in others.

I offer this book, *Edit Your Life*, as a philosophy of editing as a life practice. It is divided into three sections, which correlate with the three steps of editing anything:

Part 1: Examine Your Life provides a framework for looking with fresh eyes at your ordinary days: to understand what your life needs to be and to edit in the right direction, without accidentally changing something that works well.

Part 2: Edit Your Life offers avenues for making lasting changes according to what feels right and true to your life today, whether you are editing for clarity and ease, for growth, or for a greater sense of abundance.

Part 3: Enjoy Your Life introduces simple ways to enjoy the ordinary days and accept the exceptions: to trust that editing time is over for this particular season, and to feel content with your here and now.

I hope this book helps you discover how you might live a right-for-you, balanced life during times of both calm and crisis. May it serve as a call to examine your life: what works, what doesn't, what can be edited, and how best to implement those changes to last for good. Each chapter—each life-edit—contains several smaller ideas, grounded in both philosophies and anecdotes, along with a practical list of things to try.

You might read with a notebook by your side for brainstorming ways to apply each life-edit. Or read with a group of trusted friends, family members, or with an accountability partner with whom you can share your ideas as you go. Above all, I invite you to read with a willingness to see your life and its possibilities with an open mind.

All the life-edits in this book are quite elastic; apply them to anything. As with any tools, adapt them, stretch them, make them your own. Use the ones that feel true to you and most appealing now; the others will be there if you need them. The book is intended to be read and the life-edits tried out chronologically, though any order of using the tools will form a sort of blueprint for your life going forward. A way to trust your own decision-making, your choices of what to accept and what to change. A way to align what you love with what fills your day.

Dear reader, welcome. This book is for you. Here's to your life, both as it is now and as you wish for it to be.

Edit Your Life

PART 1

Examine Your Life

1

ASK: WHAT IS IT?

Looking Closely

Looking closely is an editor's best tool. To *revise* a thing, whether a poem or a life, means literally to look again. It is a way of creating enough distance to see clearly. Often I see a writer frustrated with a project and wanting it to be something that it's not, and the best gift a good editor can give is to point gently to what it *seems to want to be*. Only then we can find its true form.

This, then, is our work with our lives. To look at the facts as neutrally as possible, without judgment; to look again; to see the direction in which our life desires to grow; and to prune along its natural shape. To ask questions whose answers will give us good information, such as: What does it contain? What boundaries confine it? What does it feel like to live it? What are its energy sources?

When I put this idea forth—*first, just look*—to my writing students, I can see their doubts. I understand why. Labor is built into the human species. It is no surprise, then, that often we feel that if we are not solving a problem or offering critique or doing active work, we're not doing anything. Yet we are bound to edit badly unless we first take time to understand what this thing is that we have on our hands—before worrying about what it should be or imposing our will upon it.

First, just look.

Before considering any edit, I ask these three questions in order:

1. What is this trying to be or do? (What is its ideal version?)

2. What works? (How does it succeed in meeting that ideal version?)

3. What is needed? (Where are the gaps between its "now version" and its ideal version?)

Asking these questions—a formula for looking closely—is so simple, and so applicable to any situation.

PURE NEUTRAL FACTS: WHAT IS IT?

There are many ways to look closely. You can journal, or track your time, or talk to a friend. If you want to track what you eat or how much money you spend, the simplest way is to jot down these facts for a few days, then observe the patterns.

You can also get creative. Draw a picture of your day every night before bed for a week (you can do this with someone you love or live with, which might lead to a laugh!). What do you notice? Before my husband and I moved to Idaho, when we were trying to figure out where to start our businesses, with an eye for how we might both work from home and spend a lot of time with any future children, we learned a lot from the goofy task of making crayon drawings of each of our "ideal homes."

Mine was a small lively town with three-story brownstones and people smiling out of them; it had dogs, cafés, a university, a theater, a farmers market, many pedestrians, and a bookstore spanning a city block.

"Let's see yours," I said.

James turned his paper around. On it was a stick-figure picture of himself in a tent next to a mountain and a river, with no neighbors.

Through these two (badly drawn) extremes, we saw clearly that we needed to make a compromise.

Meditation does a form of this: it asks us to look at the thoughts. Meditation does not come easily to me. Journaling and crayon drawings do. Go where your water naturally flows.

Before we moved to the Shed, I felt that I didn't have much bandwidth at home for just looking—there was too much to do!—but I did notice two disquieting facts.

One was that whenever anyone spoke to me, whether a guest, my spouse, or one of my children, I tended to half listen while doing some household task: washing dishes, folding laundry, tidying up, wiping counters, cooking, rescuing toys that the dog had half eaten. Or I would eye my computer and think of all the work I should be doing. Whereas outside the house—walking, driving, playing in the yard or in a park or in a public place—I noticed that I fully listened, and therefore my best conversations and my most engaged parenting happened out in the world.

Second, I observed that in the house, I told my children no at least twice as often as I told them yes—because they were always on the brink of wreaking some household chaos or bickering over an object. Whereas out of the house, I said yes more; I encouraged them to explore and try new things. As a consequence, they behaved better when not at home. They allied themselves as friends and looked curiously at the world and its wonders; they asked big questions. I enjoyed my children's company more outside the house. I could be the parent I wanted to be.

These two were unarguable facts: I encountered them near daily in my journaling and in my conversations, and just by observing myself.

I could have berated myself for this information—after all, it doesn't reflect very well on me—but I decided to listen to it. What did it tell me?

What these facts told me is that at this point in my life, I did not have the daily willpower to resist the lure of housework, or to set clear boundaries around paid work. Or put another way, during this season in my life, work was of a magnitude that swelled in proportion to the amount of time we were in the house. I did not feel able to play until the work was all done, and—guess what?—it never was. If I wanted to be an attentive person—someone who looks back on her life and remembers doing something besides laundry and saying no—then I would need to take my conversations and the bulk of my parenting outside, to the hiking trails and parks, or to public places like museums, cafés, or libraries. Knowing this information would change my life. It would go on to shape the ideal version, the guardrails, and all the other editing tools that I will share here.

When we look, the facts we find are not good or bad: they are pure neutral facts, and we try to arrange them by how close or far they set us from the ideal self and the ideal life.

THE ART OF RETREATING TO FIND |YOU|

I have always been fascinated by people who edit in order to live their first-choice lives, even when they were already living good lives. The grandmother who runs a marathon, the attorney who pivots and writes a legal thriller, the teenager who starts a political movement, the child who starts a pet-sitting business so he can be around animals all the time. Shaping a life into its first-choice form feels like worldmaking, engaging with the godlike possibilities of our own ordinary hands. It feels in alignment with a deep, shared energy when people edit their lives toward their ideal states of being. It is the opposite of stagnant; it is a turning toward movement, growth, and life. But it is hard to see our own lives clearly while we are living them.

Here we introduce the subtle art of retreating. If you can't figure out what your first-choice life *is*, because you're stuck in the thick, ripe middle of it, try taking a retreat. This need not be luxurious. House-sit a night for a friend who is traveling. Spend a long weekend in a cousin's spare bedroom. If you can afford it, rent a room at an inn for two nights. Or longer if you like. You can also take a retreat on a micro scale: reserve half a day—or even thirty minutes—to lay your responsibilities aside. Turn your phone off; clock out from the requirements of external tasks—they will still be there when you return, and perhaps they will feel less urgent for your having retreated.

On retreat, do what you like. Walk, rest, loaf about, do things for fun. Have a meal that you like. Self-nurture. Ask, *What do I want to do?* If nothing comes up, then do nothing. Check in with yourself and see what thoughts or feelings or facts arise. If fearful thoughts arise, listen to them for a moment. Notice their common denominators. Are they speaking from fears about money or safety? About being unloved or alone? Try to hear them out as you would hear a friend. Then do your best to set them aside: Imagine yourself turning down the volume on them. You might even write them down and put them into a closed jar to open at another time. Do any exercise that you can think of to set aside any anxiety for now. You might thank your inner voices for their concern, then say that you don't need them while you are on retreat. Then do your best to get back to doing what feels good.

This small act is extraordinarily valuable, and it need not take much time out of your ordinary life. Retreating from ordinary habits and obligations will give you the chance to be absolute value |you|.

You may be wondering what in the world those lines are! Remember from school those good old math symbols that strip the positive or negative charge off a number? Whether +5 or −5, if you put it in absolute value terms, it becomes just |5|. This is what we need to find for ourselves when we strip away all the outside values.

I stumbled upon this truth a decade ago when I had a year-and-a-half-old baby. I had heard so many older mothers say that they wished they had given themselves time, even just a little time, for themselves when their children were young. They felt it would've set a good example for their children to see their mother taking care of her own needs, as well as the needs of her family. It never hurts to borrow other people's wisdoms, I figured, and so for my birthday, when my generous husband asked what I wanted, I said, "Two nights alone." Done, James said. I felt enormously fortunate to have his support. If I hadn't, though, I still think I would've tried to make a retreat happen—I would've asked a friend, a grandparent, hired a sitter, or swapped twenty-four hours of childcare with a friend.

James kept our daughter and the two of them had their own adventures, while I drove three hours to the tiny town of Stanley,

Idaho (population: 61), where I stayed in a humble rustic room with a shared bathroom down the hall. There, I spent the long days writing in the empty restaurant downstairs, where the kind hotel owner said I could help myself to hot water for tea, so I did (I always travel with tea bags). I bracketed my days with walks in the morning and late afternoon. Once I took a luscious nap. In the evenings, I wandered down to a nearby lodge to have a glass of wine, watch the sunset, and people-watch. One night I got to listen to a local band.

Throughout those three days, I began to feel restored from the intense duty and responsibility of my life at home as a young mother and teacher. I wrote forty pages of my novel in progress, thanks to the days of pure undistracted focus. I went to bed when I was tired and slept until I felt rested. I lost track of time. How long had it been since I had lost track of time? Easily years. We can all benefit so much from that feeling of shedding all commitments and just living our lives moment to moment. I knew it was not possible—or even, for all of us who live with responsibilities to others, desirable—to live in this open and unrestricted state all the time, but it felt wonderful to do for a weekend.

Also, during my retreat, I met strangers. Within three days, I met 20 percent of the town (quick math: twelve people) and had lively conversations with them, learning about their lives in a small town. It was a beautiful, productive weekend, and I came home happy to see my family and with several emotional souvenirs.

First, the retreat imbued me with confidence that absolute value |Elisabeth| needed to have writing in her day-to-day life in order to flourish.

Second, the retreat reminded me how much |Elisabeth| is given energy from random conversations with people during the day.

Based on these findings, I vowed to start waking earlier to give my novel breathing room. I decided that I'd try to reserve time in the afternoons to go into the world with my daughter: on walks, to friends' houses, to cafés, to museums, to the park, to engage in the simple pleasure of making new friends, of having random conversations, and of feeling part of a village. The balance of monastic working mornings and sociable afternoons made me feel so alive while I was on retreat—so I decided to cultivate it at home. Each year I try to repeat some version of this weekend, even if I can only manage a single day or night—as a way to reengage with myself away from home: to take my own pulse and feel what gives me energy.

Third, I realized that my people were okay when I took that time—in fact, they had an equally fruitful weekend of first choices: they fed a horse, went to Home Depot, and completed a garden project. My husband showed me a photo of our girl in her gigantic embroidered bloomers and her tiny pink cowgirl boots, holding a shovel and digging. This assuaged my parent guilt. They missed me, as I missed them. But we emerged from the weekend with energy and stories to tell each other. The weekend helped me see anew not only my own absolute-value energy givers, but theirs.

THE MAGIC: WHAT WORKS?

In both life and writing, it's tempting to dwell on what *doesn't work*. It's easier to spot, and it's certainly more annoying! This is because it distracts us from what *does* work.

When you observe your life as it is now, what works? It may be something that you take for granted: Perhaps you have people in your life around whom you can be fully yourself. Count it. Or perhaps you are healthy. Count it many times over. This is both good luck and also, perhaps, something you are doing: getting enough rest, drinking enough water, keeping stress in check, finding outlets for joy and creativity and love. Do either of these feel true? Find something that does. Look around your life until you can say with certainty a few things that are true about it and that are working well.

It might be a relationship that is innately solid, or a room in your house that feels good to be in, or a hobby that you have enough time to do. It might be something you enjoy about your job. Or it might be something very small.

One very small thing that has always worked well for my family is that we know where to put our keys, sunglasses, and wallets when we come home. Small but mighty. This means that in the course of a usual day or year, we don't lose these vital objects that we need in order to leave the house. One of my best friends set up a sacred key place after spending four hours digging in trash bins for the keys. Turns out her toddler had put them where he thought they belonged, in her sock drawer. Because I see in my own life the small but mighty benefits of having a set home for things we use frequently, I can take this further by asking myself what other "set homes" I can create for objects and events in my life. This can be applied to time: Which dates or tasks or practices should have a set home in the calendar? And this can be applied, of course, to everything else.

Think of examples in your life: Where are you sailing smoothly? What can you always find? What do you usually do with confidence? What do you make—conversation, soup, gardens, schedules, promises—that invariably turn out well? What can you be relied upon to do? Who always feels easy to be around? Which parts of your day feel simply *good*? What do you most look forward to?

What would you miss if it changed?

In short: What would you miss if it changed?

As with any lifelong practice, we must learn any useful principle again and again, always in humbling and different ways. Sometimes what works is well disguised by something that doesn't work, and herein lies the beauty of this editing tool.

This "just looking" tool was one that I forgot during the early days of the pandemic, for it seemed that my kids weren't learning anything. I was failing daily at getting them to sit down and do their schoolwork—it seemed all they really wanted to do was color the big pieces of cardboard that kept arriving from Amazon carrying virus-time staples and make them into cardboard villages. We made elaborate plans for how we'd (surely!) do better tomorrow—we'd follow the lessons the school sent. Tomorrow was invariably the same as today. Daily and hourly we failed. At last I surrendered. I made myself a cup of tea and sat on the sofa and let them do their thing. My children were building a village for their combined dozen stuffed animals, and the village required a school bus and a restaurant. They talked amiably throughout the morning, making requests of each other and sharing scissors. In watching, I saw something startling. They were collaborating to do their own creative versions of the two things I'd been failing to teach them.

> **Math:** "This side has to be twice as long as that one if we're going to make a school bus," my son advised his older sister. And she said back, "We'll have sixteen ice cream flavors. Help me cut up four cardboard shelves so we can do four on each."

> **Spelling:** From menus for their cardboard-box restaurant (primary menu item: doughnuts and ice cream—both misspelled, of course!), to invitations for all the stuffed animals, they were writing plenty on their own terms.

In short, they were independently creating the magic that I'd been trying for months to create for them. While this didn't feel like a permanent substitute for school, it helped me see that they were learning by doing. It made me more patient for the remainder of homeschooling. It reminded me—again!—that I need to remember to look closely before imposing my will.

Sometimes what is working can be found hidden beneath what isn't working—and sometimes what isn't working is us, trying to fix something that with a little space and time would resolve itself. When you survey your own life, look both for things that work with your help and things that work without it. Step back and observe. There is always something, however small, that works— and we must build around it.

THE FRACTURES: WHAT DOESN'T WORK?

When we commit to something, be it a friendship, volunteer activity, or a schedule, we can "get to good" by repeating a small positive action—saying a kind thing, exercising, listening, learning, compromising—over time. The positive layers add up, like good sedimentary rock, and suddenly your life looks as you hoped it would. Repetition goes a long way.

The flip side is true as well: not committing fully—or not knowing where to commit our time and energy—leads to fractures and confusion. When I look at my own life and locate what isn't working, it's often the places where I feel indecisive, where I'm doing the emotional splits between two or more options. Where something doesn't feel right, one of the major puzzle pieces of my life has been jammed in the wrong place. Everybody has those moments: Where you are in the wrong career but feel it's too late to change. Where you are in the wrong relationship—not seen, not heard, not nourished and loved in the ways you need. Sometimes these are fixable, sometimes not. It can hurt to look. And yet—if we wish to live deliberately—look we must.

Asking what doesn't work may bring up things from a deeper level than we currently have the power to change. There might be massive parts of your life that are not working and that you have little or no control over, and the idea of looking at any of it with an editor's eye might feel like hopeless nonsense. That's okay. Think of one small thing that you might be able to change *today*. Anything. It can be how you speak to someone in your life today—or how you speak to yourself. It can be a choice to not take the bait in an argument. It can be what you put in or on your body today. It may be even smaller.

Start there. In time, you might have more agency than you thought. But either way, you will have at least taken some control over some of the things that are in your power.

We all have experienced a disconnect somewhere in our lives when the thing we worked hard for turned out not to be something we actually wanted. We fall in love—and try hard to make it work—with the wrong person. We move cross-country for a career . . . only to find that we were happier at home. We study for months to take the LSAT . . . only to find that law school is the wrong path. We get a Labrador at the wrong time. (I have done all four of these.) In short, we raise our life to be a certain thing, and it becomes that thing—and then we wish it were something else.

This causes an obvious crisis between the ideal and the real. It makes us feel annoyed (or furious) at our crooked paths and wasted efforts. In the words of Joseph Campbell: "There is perhaps nothing worse than reaching the top of the ladder and discovering that you're on the wrong wall." But before these disconnects, there are nearly always rumbles that something feels off. We may have been moving in the right direction, but somewhere we miscalculated a step or a priority.

When you look at those disconnects, you might ask: What is always hard? What never feels right? What used to be fun but no longer is? What did you want from this experience—and is it anywhere to be found? When and where do you find yourself being the least charming version of yourself, or complaining the most? Is there one time of day—the beginning, the end, or 4:00 p.m.—when life always feels like a slog? Have any problems suddenly come about—and stayed?

This pattern is well worth noticing. One of my friends found that going to work felt painful for a year—then he realized that he had been wearing the wrong-size shoes. When he got the right size, his life felt right again. My son as a toddler went through a sudden-onset stuttering phase—which only went away when we realized that each time he tried to speak, someone interrupted him (thus he had started interrupting himself). When we let him finish his sentences, his normal speech resumed.

These are simple examples, a good place to look first. Then look at the more deep-set ones. Think of examples in your life: Where are you often frustrated? What or who constantly disappoints you? Are there any unhelpful patterns from your history or family that are still hanging around and hard to shake? What do you too often do wrong (in your own eyes or others' eyes)? In which situations do you feel the least confident? What can you *never* be relied upon to do, even if you have the best of intentions? Which promises to yourself are you likeliest to break? Who always feels difficult to be around? Which parts of your day feel simply *hard*? What do you most dread?

In short: What would you very much like to see change or resolve?

These are your fractures. Fractures may come and go, and the purpose of just looking is to see what is going on *now*. To determine whether we can heal them, or whether they will go away on their own, or whether they are not as bad as we thought, in which case perhaps we should embrace them.

CLOSE-READ YOUR EMOTIONS

Just as the physical body usually shows signs of what it needs, our emotions reflect what is hidden below. It is absolutely true that anger is a good signal—as is sadness, frustration, excitement, or contentment. A strong emotion is a sign that something is needed or desired, or that something should be avoided or handled with care. We are wise to use our analytical skills to close-read our emotions: What subtext is there?

If we feel grumpy that a friend we were supposed to meet failed to show up, is there anything else to learn from that feeling? Maybe not: we were looking forward to the date. But maybe so: maybe she consistently cancels. Or maybe we feel relieved that she didn't show up—a feeling worth investigating! If we find ourselves angry at loading the dinner dishes, ask why: Did you feel that your dinner was not appreciated? Is this a common thing? Or did you look forward to dinner as a time to connect and now you feel frustrated that it wasn't?

Whatever the feeling, we can see it as good information. We can learn from it. Eventually we can act on it. In this way, we can cycle from unproductive emotions (that trap us in undesirable places) to productive ones (that drive us toward desired outcomes).

Close-reading looks at small details as a way to get a sense of the big picture; when we close-read our emotions, we examine a feeling to try to understand what facts may have caused it. It can also help us speak what we know we need, and make us better at being empathetic to others. We can venture a guess (maybe correct, maybe not) at what they might be feeling.

Close-reading our emotions helps us both tell the truth (articulate the feeling, if only to ourselves) and do it with kindness and compassion (seeking to understand the chronology of events and patterns that may have led up to it). Also, and very importantly, such analysis helps us feel more comfortable looking at feelings straight-on, and even discussing them so they do not become taboos.

A brief word on looking closely and taboos. As with any hard work, if we spend too many days ignoring something or someone, we become afraid to look at it. We see this immediately when ordinary things become a crisis: delaying paying taxes or calling the internet provider or responding to an important letter or failing to show up for a family member or friend who needs us now. Or ignoring a small health problem until it grows too large to ignore. In the words of Annie Dillard, your work is like "a lion you cage in your study. . . . You must visit it every day and reassert your mastery over it. If you skip a day, you are, quite rightly, afraid to open the door to its room."

Life is this way. Looking away from your life is like turning your back on the ocean. It will always fell you. But keep a steady eye out, and accept that it will knock you over now and then— prepare for this, accept it with humor, and keep a nimble step. Know that nearly everything is correctable—after all, life is ongoing and we learn to edit as we go. What we see when we look closely is simply our life. These details are our details, but the fact of figuring them out links us to everybody who has ever lived. In short, don't create a personal taboo by denying the facts of your life. Accept that they are both beautiful and challenging. Look for the truth. Tell the truth. Act upon the truth. Look long enough and you will know what you have to do.

A journal can be a valuable asset for close-reading emotions—as can be a trusted person. A friend goes both ways: you can be for each other both a good cheerleader and a worthy counterargument, as you explain your lives to each other and listen well, asking thoughtful questions. Finding a friend to check in with—someone who is not your parent, child, or partner, and therefore someone whose choices you can see impartially—may help you to think critically about your life, and also to feel compassion for yourself through another's eyes. Perhaps most vitally, it helps you see where you are not stuck: to see your life as a set of choices. During one year when a dear friend in another city and I both were facing life changes, we implemented a weekly half-hour phone date, as well as a two-person book club for discussing books that we thought we could both grow from.

Such close-readings and conversations prevent us from sticking our heads in the sand when something needs to be changed. When at regular intervals we look closely at our lives, we are more likely to notice and act: to think creatively and put more choices on the table, or simply to pause and let a situation play out. We can choose to change or to accept, and we can choose to do either one with ease or with a fight. Certain times call for both. Seeing our life as a narrative that we are telling while living it reminds us we have the ability to make choices that fit the lovely and lopsided shapes of who we most deeply are.

LIFE-EDIT PROMPTS

1. **Make time for a retreat.** In any form you can, for at least half an hour, but for as long as you can responsibly take.

You can do this at home if you clear a space away from duties and distractions. If you leave home, find a humble, comfortable lodging. Or borrow a friend's space. If you live alone, swap homes for a weekend with a friend who lives alone. Feed each other's pets. You each will find space by living a different life from your own. Notice what absolute value |you| looks and feels like, when freed from your ordinary commitments.

2. **Set a life review date.** Set a date with yourself at intervals—monthly, or seasonally, or yearly—to pause and step away from ordinary routine, even just for a few hours. Go to a quiet place (cafés in the early morning work well for me—or it can be a long walk, or your office). Observe your life as it is. Reflect on each element: What is your current situation at work? In relationships? With your house and community? Writing or making lists or doodling (or crayon drawings!) may help. Simply notice what you notice, as honestly and objectively as you can. Make a list of the disconnections in your life, the not-working parts. Can you line them up with what you wish they were instead?

3. **List your hats.** Make a list of every one of your responsibilities, the many different hats you wear over the course of a year. None are too small—if you are the default dishwasher at home, write that down. Break

down your work within your family: Do you wear the hat of being the primary meal conversationalist, for instance? The mail opener and bill payer? Think of other responsibilities that come with your job—for example, a teacher is not only responsible for teaching but for out-of-class conferences, class preparation, and grading assignments. Keep this list as an ongoing (living) document—it provides a map of what your life is, in terms of the tasks you perform.

4. **Divide into energy columns.** Once you feel pretty satisfied with your hats list, make a second list, dividing all of your responsibilities into two columns: those that give you energy (energy givers), and those that deplete your energy (energy takers). Some may be neutral, but most will fit into one of the two columns, either lightly or strongly. Do you like one part of your job but not another? Whether you are an accountant, a zoologist, a pilot, or a philanthropist, my guess is that there are certain parts of the work that give you energy more than others—and this is good information. Do you enjoy certain parts of life at home and struggle with others? If you're not sure, picture yourself doing that activity— and notice if your energy rises and falls at the thought. Write it down truthfully, then assess your list. What do you notice about its balance? Where do the proportions

feel right, where wrong? Do you wish to take on more of the energy givers? Are any of the energy takers expendable or possible to outsource?

5. **Dig below your emotions.** Ask good hard "whys" about your columns. What subtext lies beneath? Do you feel a certain way while doing certain tasks or having certain conversations? Why? Observe why something may be a tender spot. What do you think is there that feels off or inauthentic or uncomfortable or imbalanced? When we close-read our emotions, we excavate hidden and useful information—including inherited "shoulds" and vulnerable feelings that we are trying to shield.

6. **Consider your inherited emotions.** Are there certain energy takers you do that you feel an inherited pressure to do? Say your dad spends hours reading the news each day, so you feel compelled to do the same, or your supervisor always responds to messages within the hour, so you feel it's the best practice? Press upon these inherited feelings: Are they useful to your life today? How? Do the opposite: Now ask what you like about your energy givers. Do you like the parts that involve management, or problem-solving, or community-building, or that you get to do in company or in silence? Do you prefer the ones that involve planning or spontaneity? Observe a few layers below

each of your tasks—what does it tell you about you? What have you inherited—from family or world—that shape this feeling? Are these inheritances that you wish to keep?

7. **Speak aloud your facts.** Find someone outside your home who can listen to you talk about these lists and discoveries. Set a date. Weekly or monthly talks with friends or accountability partners go a long way in helping you see your life accurately and helping someone else do the same. It can be as simple as you like, even a weekly one-sentence text update, a single texted heart each time you meet a daily goal, or a short call while making toast. You can share your written lists from your life-editing work with this person if you wish, but mostly just tell them what you have found. In describing your life to someone who is a neutral party to your day-to-day affairs, whether a friend, sibling, stranger, or professional counselor, you will undoubtedly articulate what your life, in essence, is. This is worth doing in pairs: Speak and listen in turn, and observe back—in pure neutral summary—what you have said aloud. Does anything about it surprise you? Does it feel like an accurate portrait of your life as it is now? Another way to do this exercise is to write a letter to yourself about what you observe.

8. **Ask: What is? What works? What doesn't work?** In your conversation, ask the person you are speaking with what they notice about what you have told them. You can also do this with yourself in a journal. The old editing questions come in handy here, and it serves to answer them as honestly as possible:

    1. What is your life today (the now version)? What is it trying to be or do (the ideal version)?

    2. What works in your life (the ways the now version meets that ideal version)?

    3. What is lacking in your life (the gaps or fractures between the now version and the ideal version)?

Once you have an accurate portrait of what your life is—what it contains, what gives you energy, and what the balance is between now version and ideal version—you have the most valuable tool for designing your life as it needs to be: you have an accurate direction for your editing.

2

ASK: WHAT COULD IT BE?

Identifying the Moonshot

One of the greatest problems that can trouble a piece of writing is not knowing which way to take it. Avoiding this albatross requires the serious work of sifting through all the possible avenues forward to determine which one makes the most sense, both for the needs of the project and the writer's skill set. There are infinite choices—and the writer must choose which one is their first-choice version. Their "moonshot."

This is no small job. Infinite choice in theory sounds intoxicating—like everyone's favorite genie wish of being granted endless wishes—but in reality, it can feel paralyzing. Modern life presents more choices than a single person can possibly handle. See this friend or that one? Pursue this job or that other one? Read which of these thousand books? This is what psychologist Barry Schwartz calls the paradox of choice. He tells a story of walking to the store to buy a pair of blue jeans, being offered hundreds of options, and walking out, overwhelmed and jeans-less.

For all the many benefits of living in a season of bounty and choice—and don't get me wrong, there are very, very many benefits—one disadvantage is that we can feel this problem of too-muchness in terms of how to go forward and what to do now. In times of change or crisis, on the contrary, people are forced to focus on a single means for survival, just one way forward—and even though we are uncomfortable or suffering, we are at least clear-eyed about it. As the editors of our lives, we can adopt this clear-eyed perspective on a regular basis by asking ourselves a single question: *What is my first choice?*

Your first choice is the one that gives you the most energy, that you are drawn innately to, and that you are willing to make sacrifices for. It is usually the intuitive choice. In determining your moonshot professionally, do not worry if your ambition is above your current skill level. It arguably should be, for this is how we grow! First choices seed the potential for growth. Growth sometimes hurts; it is the shedding of a skin. But when we prioritize first choices, we know we are growing in the direction that feels right.

Our first choice can become an organizing principle for our days and our decades. We can make decisions with this first choice in mind, so that decision-making feels deliberate and not simply like one big google. Your organizing principle might be to spend a lot of time in nature, or to be in a certain type of relationship, or to live near (or away from) certain people, or to work with ideas, or to make things with your hands, or to learn every day, or something else that feels innate to you. From an early age, I knew that my moonshot goal was to be a writer, and that I would need to organize my days to make time for writing. I would need time, space, and treats to lure me to the desk. I would need relationships that supported me and respected the bouts of daily solitude that writing requires. Knowing your first choice helps decision-making feel clear. If you need an easy gauge, ask yourself: What do you feel satisfied when you do, and growly when you don't do? What gives you energy?

It is easy to leap out and gather second choices: clothes we won't wear, books we probably won't read, friends we don't wish to take to our grave. It is a lot harder and more satisfying at the root level to read one book slowly and have it change you; to perform one task well and have it leave an impact; to commit to a small number of clothes in which you look your best; to listen deeply over the years to a few beloved people and grow from the time spent together.

Think for a moment of the energy it takes to choose a second choice. Say a mate. If you are in a relationship with someone who is not your first choice, many days you wake up and think: *Should I find someone more suitable for me? Do I love this person enough?* Every day of indecision drains us and shames us, making us more likely to settle for other second choices. Same with a job we do not love. We spend the day not learning or growing but wondering when and how to leap, chiding ourselves for wasting our potential, or brainstorming what distraction we can offer ourselves after 5:00

p.m. to survive another day. Rather than gaining energy through engagement with our lives—which is always nourishing—we find ourselves spent from our efforts to disengage.

Be aware that choosing a first choice doesn't mean choosing it all the time. In reading this now and thinking about your moonshot, you might consider what small seed changes could pack a big punch in starting your commitment to it—you can grow them later, if you wish. You have time to build support structurers to uphold what you need. The "how" will come next—for now, establish the "what." Cultivating the editing habit of choosing first choices—at a micro level at first, and then at a macro level—shifts us toward identifying and claiming the ideal version of our lives, while also seeing what in our lives is already just as we wished.

PRACTICE LOW-STAKES FIRST CHOICES

There are many low-stakes ways to apply this "first choice" principle without making major life changes. And like any skill, practice makes progress and progress makes perfect enough. Practicing low-stakes first choices helps habituate us to striving for bigger ones.

Look around your room. What in it is not your first choice? You will know immediately. Look through your clothes. Which do you want to wear tomorrow? Likely only a few. Open your cabinets. Quite likely there are a few items you appreciate daily, and many others that gather dust: Either you feel guilt at not using them, or you feel an inherited responsibility to keep them because they were someone else's first choice, once upon a time. But keeping them is fairy-tale thinking. This is your life! Gather the second-choice items and put them away for a while: those that are not beautiful, used, and loved. Observe your level of contentment without them. If you don't miss them, perhaps get rid of them for good, reminding yourself that things belong with people who love them.

That said, there are certain objects for each person that feel impossible to curate. For my husband it is fishing poles—he still has the rod he won at a competition when he was nineteen, among others that he's kept for over two decades. He told me plainly when we were dating that many of his friends were coerced by their wives to give up their fishing gear, and I solemnly swore I would never ask him to do that. I still haven't. For me, it is backpacks. It's such a dorky obsession! But I think they represent portability for me, so I continue in the holy grail search for the "backpack to rule all backpacks." You may have one of these obsessions too—forgive yourself for it, and practice first choices with something easier.

Say you are trying to eat in a certain way. Your first choice is eating healthfully, and the second choice is a cookie (which may lead to all the cookies). Fill your pantry with the first-choice foods and leave the cookies outside the house, so they do not tempt you every minute of every day. Or honor your first-choice way of eating by only eating cookies when you are sharing them with a friend, so it becomes a double treat. Or make a practice of eating a bite— just one small bite!—of something healthy before something unhealthy. My friend cured himself of a major sweet tooth by practicing the first-choice behavior of eating a handful of nuts before having any sugar. Usually after the nuts, the sweets craving lessened or went away entirely.

This "lead with first choices" principle can be adapted in a whole host of daily ways. If you want to drink more water or read more news articles, take a minute or two to drink a full glass or read an op-ed before sitting down for lunch. Go outside for five minutes before sitting down at the computer. And so on. Make the first-choice habit the portal through which you can access the ordinary habit.

You can do this the other way too, putting honey before medicine: Write the best compliment you've ever received at the top of your to-do list, or set a clip from a sweet voice recording as your morning alarm—so that the portal to your day washes you in a feeling of being loved.

Look at the activities you do with and for the people you love. Which ones are the best use of your brain and heart and body? If you are doing these activities for other people, which ones do your other people seem to most value? Are you making meals for people who do not eat them? Are you helping children with homework when they do not need it or when it results in arguing? Are you micromanaging work projects that could be an opportunity for younger colleagues to grow? Keep doing the ones your people appreciate, and let the others go. One of my friends said that she used to spend hours getting ready in order to look perfect for each event she attended with her husband, because she thought it mattered to him, yet each time they headed out the door, he seemed grumpy. Weird, she thought. After a frank conversation many years into their marriage, what she found is that he didn't care what she wore, but it bugged him that her lengthy grooming routine always made them late. Her takeaway: Wear whatever she feels best in, and get to the party on time.

Look at your calendar. What in it is not your first choice? What in your day feels like it is not the best use of your time and your unique and individual set of loves and skills? Bow out of second-choice recurring events if you can. Say that you need to reevaluate your time commitments; you will take a break for the summer and see how you feel come autumn.

I overheard my children having a conversation about first choices after a night at a restaurant, when they had been sent home with crayons. Scott was trying mightily to stuff them into his art kit, a hefty zippered pouch that he keeps in his backpack. Cora has broken enough zippers in her life to be able to confidently advise her brother not to stuff his art pouch full. Still he tried to close the bulging bag. She tried a different tactic: "Do you like these art supplies as much or more than your others?" Scott hesitated. He had just gotten new markers the previous week. "No," he said honestly, and left the crayons on the table. Cora examined them and decided to take just the yellow one for her own kit. She added her wise final word as big-sister authority on crayons: "If you practice first choices in your art kit, you will practice them in your whole life."

Living in a tiny house forces the first-choice habit. My closet in the bedroom loft is a horizontal peg, about six inches long, that can fit roughly eight hangers—enough for a week's worth of dresses. My husband has the same, and each child has a deep drawer with six sections. This allows us eight outfits each, and we do laundry once a week. We can only wear first choices, clothes we love and feel great in. As Elizabeth Cline observes in *The Conscious Closet*, better to have a few well-made items you love and wear all the time than a full closet that you feel ho-hum about. This requires us all, even the children, to decide when it is time to replace our clothes. In the bin we keep in our garage for out-of-season clothes, we still have to be discerning, for a bin can only fit so much. Ditto the first-choice cutting board. The first-choice pantry goods. The first-choice silverware. The first-choice books and toys (but not—god forbid—fishing poles or backpacks!).

When a first-choice object wears out or no longer serves its purpose, you donate it and replace. When a first-choice friend or mate is unhappy, you take time to repair what has gone wrong. You devise systems so this unrest won't repeat. You replace old systems with new ones. By refusing second choices on a small scale, you begin shifting toward first choices on a large scale. In short, a daily practice of choosing first choices will benefit all the choices we make, great and small.

What if you find that you have made the wrong first choice? There is always a way to backtrack or patch up the path you've skidded away from.

With people, of course, it helps if we leave workplaces and relationships kindly, offering as much gratitude and grace as we can muster, and if we can avoid badmouthing that which we have left. But remember that a leap in a first-choice direction is a brave thing to do, something worth admiring, something that inspires others— and something that, should you find yourself negotiating with your old roommates or your old boss to take you back after you fled the nest, can be handled with a combination of diplomacy, humility, and humor.

With financial choices, it helps to try to leave a safety net for ourselves to fail and still land gently. You can work your way back to first choices too, even if it takes time and sacrifices. Upon finding himself in a job that he knew would never allow him to save, one of my friends rented his coworker's pantry, sleeping on a mattress on the floor and saving a tremendous amount of money that would've otherwise gone to rent and furnishings. After two years, he moved out of the pantry to a house of his own. (This man, by the way, is six feet four!) For him, his moonshot goal (owning a house) sustained him through a short-term (arguably last-choice!) way of living, to emerge on the other side with a sense of his own grit, a closer relationship with that friend, and a house to show for it.

When the Shed was being constructed on a little lump of grass in our backyard the summer I was pregnant with Cora, I was drunk with power at getting to choose the colors. The aqua floor was a brilliant first choice. My initial first-choice idea to paint the walls pale yellow, not so brilliant. James observed, and the builder and architect and I agreed, "It looks like a clown has exploded in here." The walls quickly got repainted off-white.

THE VERB THAT MAKES YOU FEEL ALIVE

In this life-edit, you will be scratching for something specific: the action that makes you feel most alive. I feel most alive when rapt by a sentence or a story (either reading or writing it—doesn't matter), or when deep in a conversation (it can be with someone I know well or a stranger—both feel satisfying). These two things amount to the same thing: words. I love teaching because it links writing with conversations, and therefore contains both. When I ask myself what words represent in the logic of my life, I know the answer innately: they connect. Written words connect me to people in the past and future; spoken words connect me to people right now. The verb that makes me feel most alive, then, is *to connect.*

Take a moment to reflect on this for yourself: Scrape away to find that alive thing, that first choice, pruning away what keeps it from the sunlight. What lights you all up?

What lights you all up?

Your first choice is a verb (play with children; write books; swim; play tennis; engage in meaningful conversations; explore in nature; build villages out of cardboard; sew dresses; practice medicine; make art; nurture the sick). Try it out and see which verbs give the most meaning to your life. The idea is that we live our whole life better if we place this first-choice verb at our life's center. My children's verb these days is *to craft*—I have to drag them away from their projects to get them to eat! My husband's is to swim: He loves being in training for some big swim (most recently it was the freezing twenty-one-mile English Channel—the madman!). Swimming most days makes him a more organized worker, a more patient spouse and father, and it keeps his body exercised. Win-win-win.

The further we reach down and the more we practice choosing first choices, a deeper, harder question becomes necessary to ask: Are the people you spend time with worthy of your love? Do they make you feel connected, happy, and alive? Do they support your most vital verbs? If so, root down further in your love for them. If not, reconsider whether the relationship is a balanced one. Weigh what you give and what you receive. Think back to the true friends you have had in the past, or the ones you have now. Try connecting with them.

A similarly high-stakes question may arise: Does the work you do to earn your keep on earth (whether paid or unpaid) make you feel alive? Does it challenge your heart and brain? Does it support and nourish your ideal life? Do you love it enough to sacrifice for it? If yes, then mentally renew your commitment to it and keep it buzzing right next to your heart. If not, then reconsider if it is the best choice. Even if there are no other choices at hand right now, you have made a commitment to begin looking, to begin creating in yourself a new possibility.

THE PAINLESS LONG SHOT

This one is a gift from my mom, a great believer in the idea of pursuing what she calls "the painless long shot": Apply to the best school program—they might take you! Send your work to the best editors—the worst they can say is no. Ask your first-choice crush on a date—rather than wait around for a backup crush to invite you. Drive to the front of the venue and look for any unoccupied parking spots—you may be surprised.

In painless long shots, one key is to trust that the first choice is the right choice, even if it doesn't know it yet. The other key is to accept the very real possibility of rejection. Even if your painless long shot rejects you once, twice, it still might come around in a surprising way. I have countless stories of rejection, and I promise not to subject you to all of them here. Being a writer, in my experience, means hearing no about 95 percent of the time. You get used to it pretty quickly. What I have found as a painless long shot pursuer is that every time I have felt strongly that something was a first choice—a boy I had a crush on at sixteen because he had a cute smile and a philosopher's soul; teaching college writing; spending days with children; living a portable life; publishing books—when I kept my eye on that choice, it never came in exactly the form I predicted, but it did come. The boy I had a crush on at sixteen I re-met a decade later, and now we have babies and I dedicate books to him. It was a checkered path, but isn't everything?

This is something I often hear about from my older friends, who observe that, again and again, when they missed an opportunity in their youth to do the thing they loved most—be it creating art, nurturing children, or nesting in a home of their own—that missed first-choice opportunity came back in another, wholly surprising form. Women who wanted children but did not have them later on became aunties or adoptive mothers or even Miss Rumphius–type figures in their neighborhood; creative people who found unexpected outlets—wine making, furniture making, gardening and farming, creation of businesses or simply creative lives; those who wished for mentorship or sisterhood found it, just not where they had expected. It is worth looking in your own life for examples of this. Water finds a way. So do first choices.

Water finds a way.
So do first choices.

One sweet and humble first choice that I've long cherished is to go for runs with my daughter, as my mother used to do with me. My mother would lure me out of bed, milky latte in hand, and guide me into my running shoes. I became a runner as a young woman because of her, and I thought if I ever had a daughter, I'd initiate her into morning runs. But the habit never caught on with my own girl—both because she is so much faster than I am and because these days—if I am fully honest with myself—I vastly prefer walking to running. Then recently, my daughter and I discovered something brave that we both were interested in trying:

going for cold swims. We kept hearing about people doing short exhilarating dips in natural bodies of water (like the Boise River nearby our house), and the idea intrigued us both. For a week, we summoned our courage, packed chocolate and tea to warm up with afterward, and tried it—and then for a season, we got hooked! It was not the running I expected, but a shared thing that was truly the goal. I will keep looking for further ways for that moonshot to enact itself as a form of connection with her.

My most unlikely first choice I set at age twenty-one, when I graduated from college with an English degree and no clear career prospects. I told my friend Noah my painless long shot: that one day I would teach at Harvard. "Sure, you will," he said, indulging me with a half-smile. For a decade living in Texas and Idaho, I taught anywhere that would give me a job, working toward a PhD while I did. I taught tenth grade. I taught community college. I taught writing workshops in my backyard while mothering a new baby. I did my best, but I had no steady job, and no published books. I was a bit of a sitting duck when a mentor called me up and asked me to help her with some work, which I did. Afterward, she asked: "Are you getting all the work you need to sustain yourself? Any chance you might want to teach a class for Harvard Summer School?" The following summer I spent six weeks in Cambridge wheeling the baby's stroller over redbrick sidewalks before my evening classes. It was pure magic. I went on to teach an array of writing courses for adults at Harvard Extension School, and I still do. It was not the path that I expected (I had in mind corner offices and tenure), but it was the moonshot goal enacted in a beautiful and surprising way that was just right for this era of balancing the triangle of writing, mothering, and teaching. Likewise, I had a lot of crushes between age sixteen and reuniting with my now husband in our late twenties. We claimed each other as first choices when we were both ready.

We are wise to identify our moonshots as early as we can, so we can keep them in mind and try to tread toward them, rather than spending decades doing work that doesn't light up our souls. By courting painless long shots, we allow ourselves the hope for an opportunity to greet our first choice. And we try again, and again: smarter and grittier each time. If the worst is simply ending up where we are now, then there is no reason not to try.

YOUR MODEL FIVE

The best place to see what is possible for a life is to look around you. There are so many examples of good, deliberate lives to be found. People who seem in sync with themselves, at ease with their choices, able to steer in the direction that suits them.

These are your models. Pick five to observe.

I find it useful to observe in my immediate environment first—then look back through history. Obviously, what worked for the Stoics will probably not work for me—for one thing, they didn't have to set guardrails on how many email checks they'd do each day—but still there is something to be learned from anyone who seems to be living in accordance with their truth.

What I look for are people who seem calm, at ease, and like they swim through their days like a quick freshwater fish. Nimble. Happy. Grateful. Enjoying the water. What do you look for? Whatever it is will feel authentically *good*. Will not be trying to be something, but will simply *be* that thing. No life will be perfect or seem perfect (and if it does, you might not trust it, for chaos and challenge are part of life).

And—less fun but equally useful—look to the other side. Omit this second step if it feels uncomfortable or judgmental. I think of it as good information. Which lives would leave you perpetually overwhelmed or unsatisfied? My life would not work for many. One of my friends tells me regularly that living one single day in my life would leave her feeling nerve-shot for at least a month. I believe her! What qualifies as a satisfying life, to you, is equally as important to define as what defines an unsatisfying one. We learn both from what attracts and repels us. This is your research. Just as writers find their way by reading books they both admire and cannot stand, a life-editor will find a way through studying lives.

Whose schedules excite you? I am drawn—simply by my own genetics, my love of a good sunrise, and my tendency to lose 90 percent of my charm after 9:00 p.m.—to schedules that use early mornings well. My heart starts skipping beats when I meet writers who rise at four (something I've tried but simply have not been able to pull off). But you could look at those lives and think, *Yuck! They have no nightlife!* And you could be correct.

I found that a lot of the women I looked up to, who seemed to navigate with ease the season when their children left home, had two children. Nothing magical about that. I come from four, as does my husband. Four seemed in theory like the right number. But the more I studied how my wise role models transitioned into letting their children find their own ways, the more I thought that two felt like enough for me. One child for each hand, to bring along on our explorations of the world. To replace self and husband. The insights we gain from studying models can be small or large.

Furthermore, I learned through this exercise that many people I admire balance loyalty and generosity alongside an unapologetic tending to their own needs. Their inner and outer lives feel balanced in just proportions. From these people, I've gleaned a great truth: *Selfish* is not a bad word. You can take good care of yourself and also take good care of others. I have my model five (and my model ten, and model fifty—it keeps growing!) as my proof.

Selfish is not a bad word.

Yours will be different from mine and from everyone else's. I have many dear friends whose goals are as opposite from mine as can be. We could look at the same life and I could think, *Yes!* and you could think, *Never, ever, ever!* This is fine. It is your life that we are editing here, not your friend's.

A related concept to the model five is one that a nurse friend explains to me as the "triangle of care." When identifying the right medical decision, it is important to weigh three things: the patient as a unique individual, the experienced care provider who knows (and is trusted by) the patient, and the prevailing science on the issue. Between these three, we look for the answer. Deferring to one point blindly without consulting the others disregards an important part of the triangle. In our lives, we have the same option. We have our unique absolute-value selves; we have our mentors and trusted friends; we have books and wisdom and models to offer what feels like an objectively good tried-and-true way. Try lining these three points up. What do you find in the middle? Where do they all concur—where do you have to get creative or find your own compromise? Which models work well enough— requiring you to make a few changes?

Always we must leave room for the fact that there will be certain moves you make—for us, moving into the Shed was this way—that you will have no exact model for. But this exercise still holds, because you are studying lives to understand how you want yours to look, act, behave, and feel. You can make structural changes—great and small, utterly familiar and brand spankin' new—once you have gleaned this self-knowledge first.

THE SWEET SPOT: OFTEN LESS THAN YOU THINK

A funny fact about life is that it generally feels better to long for more of something than feel annoyed with it and want less of it.

Think of a person: If you miss your friend, for example, there is a sweetness to the feeling. It is simple and pure. Compare that to the feeling of having spent too long with that same friend and wanting to end your time together but not knowing how to say so nicely. If you long for the taste of something, say a cappuccino, it is a more pleasant feeling than a stomachache from having drunk too many cappuccinos in a row. To long for more work time feels lovelier and more productive than to be at work and sick of it. One person is content with a whole long day with people—that is a sweet spot. Someone else needs an intense burst of connection, then a break.

There is a sweet spot for everything. Even though most people don't love housework, a little housework (to me, anyway) feels good: the folding of warm laundry, the creative concoction of a dinner, the making of a bed with fresh sheets, the wiping clean of a mirror. But if I am doing all these things day after day with no respite and without other people helping, I start to get annoyed.

We can choose a first choice without choosing it all the time, or even for a lot of time. People are sometimes afraid to commit to something (a stretching routine, an ambitious project, a phone call) because we wonder how we could possibly have the time! But the fact is that each one of those examples can happen in under twenty minutes. Often, we need less of something than we think.

I've seen long-distance marriages in couples who are deeply in love, who live independent lives and call each other every night and visit each other every month for a long weekend. It's not what we typically think of when we think of domestic bliss and harmony. Yet it works. An artist I know moved from Boise to San Francisco to be near the pulse of the art scene. He brought his furniture, his cat, and all his huge canvases. He moved back after one month. It was simply more than he could afford. He felt first like a failure. But he found, after testing his first-choice city, that while it felt like an avenue to his true first-choice activity (making art), it was actually not his best path. His sweet spot was a smaller city whose arts council regularly gave him generous grants. That way, he could make art all day, then afford to fly to bigger cities three or four times a year for shows. There are always ways to supplement life with the things you need for the first choice to stay alive. If you can think of it, you can probably figure out how to do it, adjusting as you go so that you can honor the sweet spots in your first-choice life.

A final word on first choices: Not only do second and third and fourth choices take up energy that can help us succeed in our first choice, but they also require a lot of stewardship. Even the clothes you do not like have to be washed and stored somewhere. Even the meals you do not enjoy or feel well after eating must be digested by your body—they use its energy. In writing, this is so clear it hurts. When part of a chapter isn't any good, I can either write something new—which takes X amount of time—or spend weeks trying to salvage it, trying to write something new but then stopping—trying to rearrange the chapter so that the second-rate part can maybe belong. You can probably imagine how well *that* goes. It is time-consuming, discouraging work, and more often than not, it fails.

First-choice thinking is an unpopular thing to do in our culture today: Think how many businesses would fail because nobody wants to do those jobs. Think how many factory foods would not be made, shipped, and eaten, because our body knows that those are not our first-choice foods. When we distill to our first choices, we gain energy because we know what we want and need. When we clutter our lives by collecting backup plans and objects, courting the opinions of people who don't matter to us, it exhausts us. When exhausted, we miss what matters.

By looking closely at what makes you feel most alive and setting your moonshots around it, first choices will distill and become clear. Soon, like anything, this sort of seeing will become a habit.

LIFE-EDIT PROMPTS

1. **Make a first-choice-verb equation.** State in a single verb what you need to be doing regularly in order to flourish: absolute value |you| = happiest when _____.

2. **Notice your safety nets.** Look around your life and observe its safety nets. What are they keeping you safe from? Some nets are absolutely necessary—leave them be! Are any keeping you safe from something that would actually be good for you, an opportunity for growth? Do you feel you can live freely knowing they are below you, or do any of them feel like they've started to hamper your choices or replace what they were put there to allow? For

example, an accountant friend took freelance tax-season work as a safety net while his own business grew—and then once his business was self-supporting and strong and needed his full-time attention, he let the safety net go. What might happen if you shed one of your safety nets? Where might you feel braver if you added one?

3. **Set your painless long shot.** If you could describe your life in its ideal version, what would it be? How would you feel? What would you be, have, and do? Your ideals are not going to be the same as anybody else's. Your "enoughs" are unique to you. Draw from your self-knowledge to think through the specifics of your own painless long shots in home, love, work, and play.

4. **Make a dot-to-dot map.** This is a silly playful game—or is it? When I think back to my husband's and my crayon drawings of our perfect place to live, it became a lodestar for our future choices, a lens for making decisions that suited us both. Draw a dot for your life as it is today—then a dot for your painless long shot. What steps between could set you up to succeed in getting there? Brainstorm a bunch of dots that might go in the middle. For example, if your dream is to be a lawyer and currently you work in customer service, one of those dots would need to be going to law school (there are night classes for this; you could still keep your day job);

another dot would be prioritizing regular study time; and another still might be finding mentors and allies in the legal field. Be creative and be specific. Which is the simplest dot-to-dot path between your "now life" and your ideal life? Which steps feel easy, which daunting? Break your dot-to-dot map into smaller steps if you need to, until each dot feels—if not easy—at least achievable.

5. **Set your sweet spot.** Ask yourself—and answer honestly—which parts of your life and work are easiest to love. What is the quality about them that makes them feel simple, refreshing, nourishing, inspiring, *good*? In which amounts do these pleasures feel best? Simply by noticing this, you will start to bask in them more—and perhaps you will notice ways to adjust harder-to-love scenarios to find their sweet spots. To take this a little further, list several of your first choices in the arenas of work, love, play, and health, and consider how long you enjoy doing them—creating a visual representation of your pleasures and their sweet spots. Is there a point of diminishing returns? What do you observe?

6. **Observe your model five.** Pick five lives—from any time and place, real or fictional—that appeal to you, and list a few reasons why. These are your model five. When thinking over questions about your own life, you can look to these to answer your questions. Think broadly

and creatively—and don't let this overwhelm you. Pick one thing that this exercise inspires and try it out for a week. It can be as simple as admiring someone who really savors weekends. My cousin is this way: when I think of her, I remember to sip my coffee slowly and indulge (even for five minutes) in *il dolce far niente*. Remember that a life-edit can be small. Don't think about changing everything; simply think of changing something.

7. **Try out the "triangle of care" exercise.** Pick any area of your life that you seek to improve or heal, and balance out what you know of yourself with what your trusted friends or mentors would say, with what conventional wisdom or an expert suggests. What feels right?

3

ASK: WHAT IS NEEDED?

Claiming What's Necessary and Discarding What's Not

Once, on a day when my children were playing quietly, I found myself checking my phone every few minutes to see if anyone had messaged me. I was in that limbo zone that parents go into when children play well: you dare not interrupt them, but you know if you get involved in anything interesting, like a book, you'll be interrupted.

In a flash, I knew what I needed: a label maker. I made a small label that read in all caps: IS IT NECESSARY? I stuck it on my phone case. For the rest of that day, I left my phone alone. It meant that that day and others, I read a magazine and made scones during my parenting downtime, which meant that I learned some new things and made something creative (and delicious), even if interrupted.

The sticker offered a way of solving two problems at once: It got me doing more things I enjoyed, and it got me checking email less.

It was clear that this reminder vastly improved my parenting. If I felt tempted to micromanage my five-year-old when she taught her toddler brother how to put on his pants, or jumping up to do a random task, I'd stop and ask: *Is this necessary?* And the answer was usually no.

The sticker's magic applied to everything: My phone case doubles as a wallet, and seeing IS IT NECESSARY? each time I pick up my wallet is a good reminder that sometimes it is (spontaneous Indian buffet lunch with my husband) and sometimes it isn't (an additional bathing suit when I live in a wintry landlocked state). The sticker kept me honest. It made me stop and think.

While I had intended for the sticker to curb my desires to do things that I shouldn't be doing (mindless email checks, buying anything that is dry-clean only, filling up between meals on sugary snacks), I discovered many valuable things that the IS IT NECESSARY? sticker urged me to do. I wish to look back on my life as a writer and remember that most days I wrote. So even if I'd rather take the day and do something else, is doing some writing necessary? Yes, usually. Even if it's bad and nobody reads it but me? Yes. Yes.

And even if my kids are misbehaving and I am about to lose the plot and it's bedtime, should I still read them books? I don't say yes to everything, but I try to say yes to that. It's necessary to the parent I want to be.

Sometimes people notice the sticker on my phone. For a long time, I traveled with extras—they were fun to share. One woman who works at the grocery store put a sticker on her steering wheel.

"These words helped me stop obsessing over my ex while I drove to work," she told me.

In the busyness of everyday life, it is hard to remember what our ideals are and what work we must do to create scaffolding for those ideals to exist. It is necessary to ask the question of what is necessary. I find that in certain eras of trying to get into a good habit, it is necessary to have some reminder, however small, tacky, or temporary, to make minute-by-minute choices that align with our values. Having to face the daily question of "Is it necessary?"—which can be reframed any way you see fit, such as "Is it useful, kind, or a source of joy right now?"—has become a frequent external reminder of the promises I make to myself, and a reminder to keep them.

YOUR NEEDS VERSUS WHAT IS AVAILABLE

When you edit your life, you think for yourself about what is necessary and what will make your life richer, lovelier, and most aligned with your true nature. This is not easy. We live in a time and place that spends a great deal of money on advertising, which presents a want as a need, and it can do so brilliantly. It bids for our attention and taps into our collective insecurity about whether we, and our life, are enough, so we fall prey to other people's definitions of what is necessary for us.

Very little, it turns out, is actually indispensable. Moments of crisis realign us because they teach us that. In a pandemic, when you cannot go into the world as you once could—and when home feels like a trap for some people, and a lost luxury for others—we are all wise to ask: What is essential?

Enough money to live modestly. Food. Water. Sleep. Movement for the body. A few people you love. Green space or some form of nature. Projects, pastimes, or activities you can do at home.

We who have all that we need are beyond fortunate. Yet it is easy to take our needs for granted, to undervalue that which we grow used to. Want is relative, but need should be clear. This is why having a practice of asking "Is it necessary?" can be a great tool and a north star.

What is essential?

We set ourselves up for crisis—both personally and at a societal level—by failing to ask this question.

Not a lot is necessary for most people, but infinite choices are available today, and we must sift through them on a daily basis. Yet throughout history, humans—even in the complicated middle of life, where I stand—have dwelt in cozy dens and caves, in huts and tiny apartments, in small dwellings of all kinds, with few luxuries. People expect to live snugly and economically in college dorms, retirement homes, and in urban centers. Many people go camping on weekends to sleep in a thin flappy tent, and this is considered recreation. Our Shed, while small, contains luxuries that our ancestors never dreamed of: electricity, instant hot water, an indoor toilet and shower, and our own clean, comfortable beds.

Even the bare minimum of what we today would call "necessary" would be seen, by our ancestors and by many people worldwide, as unimaginable luxury.

For comparison's sake, my grandfather, a Ukrainian coal miner's third child, who was born in 1915 and died in 2019, lived most of his childhood in a series of one- and two-room cabins, which he described as "quite comfortable." Many people live in similarly small spaces, even in urban, well-to-do areas. Many, if not most, Americans, however, strive to live larger, and we protect our stuff-filled homes with burglar alarms, cameras, and guns, afraid of what we could lose. But the things we can actually lose?

Not necessary.

When you think about it, most objects that can be stolen from us can be edited out with ease. They nearly all can be replaced, or the memory of them, if they are irreplaceable, can be honored. The necessary, core parts—attention, growth, knowledge, relationships, self-trust, and the like—we can only lose if we choose to neglect them.

An excess of money, time, space, luxury, and ambition does not make a person content. Again and again, researchers find that we are happiest when we have the ability to tend to our basic survival needs (both absolute survival and subjective cultural needs, like college), our comforts, and a few luxuries. In short, studies that track human contentment find that we enjoy our lives most when we have enough, plus a little extra. But when we go beyond that, happiness decreases and we find ourselves overwhelmed, burdened, and worrying about our possessions. Vicki Robin and Joe Dominguez, authors of *Your Money or Your Life*, observed that "the American Dream led us to believe that we might enjoy an ever-higher standard of living without giving up anything we already had." But, they noted, research across the board suggests that even with such abundance, "we aren't any happier." There is a cost. There is always a cost—whether in expectations, time, management, stress, distraction from our people, or weight upon the earth.

In research studying the lives of centenarians—people who are healthy and flourishing at age one hundred or older—one recurring theme is that they can identify "enough" in terms of activity, food, objects, and more, and they stop there. In Okinawa, where an astounding percentage of people live healthfully beyond age one hundred, there is even a saying before meals: *Hara hachi bun me*, translating to: "Let me stop eating when I am 80 percent full."

We can ask this of any area in our lives, to dictate what feels like our "enough."

FAVOR NIMBLENESS OVER COMPLICATION

It is unarguable that life today is more complicated than it's ever been before in terms of our physical objects, our possessions—our houses and the things we keep inside them. Once upon a time, our objects, food, and weapons were necessary to keep us alive and safe. These tools were harder to obtain. Now they are easier to come by, but often—especially if at some point in our lives, we have gone without—we still feel we need a lot of them: a big pantry for a lot of food, a big closet for a lot of clothes, many different rooms in which to play out our lives. In many cases, this makes perfect sense: If we have ever known any form of scarcity, it is natural to over-consume and over-purchase, even after we have enough.

But it is worth asking what we gain by having too much. By shedding what do not need, what fears might we shed too—and what courage or clarity might we gain in its place?

In my lifetime alone, the average home size has increased by one thousand square feet, while the average family size has shrunk. In my lifetime too, corporations have become behemoth monopolies, with fewer regulations. Our country once favored the little guy, the mom-and-pop endeavor, but not so anymore: Now we have mega-stores to take their place, saving us money but removing any relationship between buyer and seller, and chipping away at our sense of human connection. We buy and discard much, often without thought.

And for this too-muchness, we all are suffering. Bruno Latour, French philosopher and sociologist, describes an event that happened at the 2015 United Nations Climate Change Conference in which the delegates "realized with alarm" that the sum of their countries' modernization plans "would need several planets" instead of merely the one that we all share. When our ambitions for our lifetimes overrun the world we will leave behind, we are prioritizing self above all the billions who come after us—a way of leaving the world worse than we found it, just before we bow and make our exit.

The more complicated our lives become, the less nimble. There are, for each of us, daily complications that we might surrender and let go of. We are wise to think of our lives in terms of our resilience and our fluidity, rather than fixating on our barriers. When we trust ourselves to be nimble, we know our lives can change as we need them to. We can view our disappointments and failures as hiccups in the grand scheme of things, so we may move beyond them.

Asking "What is necessary?" and seeking the simpler way when facing a choice reminds us that we're not on earth to make things complicated and to obtain all that we can. Such wisdom helps us remember that editing, after all, is just finding the right shape so that the cohesive whole works—not perfectly, but well enough to be enjoyed without leaving a mess for others to clean up.

YOUR FILTER FOR THE NECESSARY

When I travel through the world today, I have a filter for the necessary that our edited life has given me. I know what is for me and what isn't. The Shed did this. When you cannot fit everything that tempts you into the square footage of your house, you learn fast to be tempted by a lot fewer things. I can walk down a city street, people-watching, observing the marvels that humans have made. But I do not feel beckoned by the signs advertising things that do not fit in my life. I filter them out.

During the writing of this book, I met my parents in Rome. "Soak everything up!" said my friend Laura, a former Italian tour guide. I translated her advice through my lens: I love walking, words, and food. Therefore, what was necessary for me to soak up Rome was to walk the beautiful crooked streets and across all the bridges; to hear a lot of people speaking the language and to try to learn a few words; to sample as much of the food as possible, especially the gelato. Rather than trying to do everything, I'd use these few avenues—curated to the things I have the most receptors to appreciate—as a way to learn about a new place.

My souvenirs were a few Italian words; a hand gesture that I love that involves both arms swooping out like twin long birds from the center of the body—a slightly exasperated way to say, "How should I know?!"; a greater understanding of the city's streets and stories; and one new friend, whose husband drove the taxi that brought me from the airport, and with whom we later spent two fun days. My filter of the necessary helped me enjoy a vacation with my parents in a way that felt fun and not overwhelming. Honing a filter of the necessary—a lexicon of my own value system—made travel choices easier and clearer.

A filter of the necessary becomes clear when we have more objects than we have space, or more obligations than we have time. In the Shed, each family member has half of a small drawer for personal care products. It means that, for this era, I choose to forgo makeup and any appliance that changes the texture of my hair. My personal-care lens for this era is "go as natural as possible." I mentioned this to a dermatologist friend, who said that really the only thing needed on the skin is water and, if you wear makeup or sunscreen, some gentle oil and a soft washcloth to wipe it off. This vastly distilled my skin-care regimen, which before that had dozens of bottles and creams—and my skin looks the same as it always did.

If you cook a lot, you need good kitchen supplies—but probably not as many as you think. If you play a sport, you need equipment— but probably not new ones until the old ones stop working or fitting. If you host a lot, by all means, you will need spare sheets—but perhaps not so many extras. Self-knowledge leads to a clear lens of your necessary to navigate your way through the world.

THE LEXICON OF LUXURIES

I find it helpful to keep this model in mind when thinking about what to me feels like a worthwhile luxury:

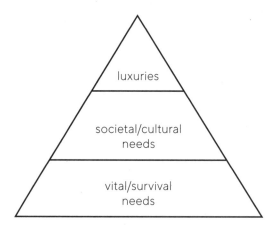

For the bottom level, we all are the same.

The middle and top levels are where it gets interesting. Depending on where you live, in the middle level it may be necessary for you to go to college or learn a trade; be independent or interdependent with a small community; know how to order out or know how to cook; have a phone or have a garden. You get the picture.

At the very top, it's a free-for-all. Each individual's luxuries will sound unarguably ridiculous to everyone else. Everywhere he goes, my dad travels with at least a dozen tour-guide books and only one pair of shoes. Everywhere she goes, my mom travels with coffee. Even to Rome, perhaps the world capital of good coffee, she brought bags of cold-brew concentrate and a handheld milk frother. My friend Dar always travels with her slippers. My tiny son cannot imagine traveling without his chess set, my daughter without more books than she can read, so she won't risk running out. Both kids require their art kits. Even to cold places, I always bring a bathing suit just in case there is a place to dip. I rarely need it, but still. The point being: If you can carry and afford it and—vital point here—if it doesn't cause real trouble to anyone in the universe, including yourself, then by all means, enjoy your luxuries.

Whatever lies on the outside of this triangle is unnecessary.

A friend asked me once how my life would change if I had unlimited means. The answer came out of my mouth before I could even think: "I'd keep my life exactly as it is, except I'd get massages each week and eat berries each day." This got a laugh out of my friend, but it was true. "You wouldn't get a new car?" she asked. Nope. I like our beaten-up Volkswagen just fine. Cars are not interesting to me except as tools to carry people. I will always buy cars that are safe and used—and ideally that someone else (my husband, who likes cars) picks out. But reflecting later on my answer, I realized that I could prioritize those two luxuries in my life a bit more.

It is worth considering what always feels like a good investment to you—and what never does. And leaving a little room for "luxury" if you can in the areas with the most payoff.

THE BARGAIN AND THE SACRIFICE

When my children started at a new school, I made friends with a single mother who never went to college. She worked serving lunch at the elementary school and once confided in me at morning drop-off that she'd always wanted to be a family counselor. *Aha!* I thought. Her painless long shot! Her first choice!

I asked her questions about what it would take. She had already looked into it. The tuition was less than she'd expected and she had enough savings, and her parents were happy to have her and her two kids come live with them to save on rent and help with childcare. "But I don't think I can do the schoolwork," she said. "I'm no good at school." You might not be anymore, I said. You're older now. You know what you want to do with your degree. Read a few books by family counselors, I suggested. Just apply and see what happens. You can wake up early to do the coursework, and work while your kids are at school.

She applied—and got in—and pulled the plug. For her, it was not worth the extra work and the disruption to the current state of her life. In short, she felt the benefit was not worth the cost. She felt that the geometry of her life would collapse if she made this change.

Fair enough. Life is a devil's bargain. Something must give to make way for something else. Christopher Vogler wrote: "A Hero is someone who is willing to sacrifice his own needs on behalf of others, like a shepherd who will sacrifice to protect and serve his flock. At the root the idea of Hero is connected with self-sacrifice." To be the hero of our own life, we have to do what makes us feel alive—those around us will benefit from it, as will we; we will add to the green of the world. But we must accept some losses. What we love, we will sacrifice for. If we love many things, we will sacrifice a little bit of all of them to keep the others afloat. Some sacrifice is always necessary if we are living consciously.

As editors of our own lives, we must constantly moderate the question of what we are willing to give up to get what we want. Depending on your attachment to that thing, it might not feel like a big deal at all. For my family, giving up a big house was a piece of cake, considering all that we got in return. I have heard many people say the same, such as a banker friend who sold house and car in order to start a healthcare business. "It was the easiest decision in the world, and so worth it," she said. But not everything is worth it, and everyone's system of worth and need is different. Sometimes our life choices are guided by what we can and cannot bear.

Often, we default to making decisions based on a single indicator: it might be money or status, both shorthand for a floor of security. Or we choose what feels immediately easiest—shorthand for a different form of safety.

Here are some bargains I have made:

> Choosing interesting work that is not very well paid because I enjoy it and learn from it.

> Commuting for work or school when the commute can be made pleasant (conversation, audio books, public transportation).

> Living in a smaller house that is closer to the activities I choose to engage in.

These are some of the bargains that I feel right about. What are yours?

When weighing any option, we must keep our first choices and moonshots in mind. What is gained must be worth more in our own value system than what is sacrificed. A friend who was an Olympic athlete and wished to continue high-level sports reinvented herself to have a stable job with benefits when she had children. This made sense; her values changed. A professor friend gave up tenure to serve as his father's caretaker and work more hours on an ambitious book project than he could while teaching. This made sense too; his values needed space to grow. A lawyer friend reduced her hours to twenty a week of solo practice so she could get a creative writing master's degree and spend more time with her sons. She took a financial hit, but it was worth it. There is a cost. There is always a cost. The question is whether the cost is worth it to our goals.

After my first two-night writing retreat when my daughter was so young, I found that I could not bear not writing—or put in the positive, writing was necessary to me—so I made the hard decision to enroll my tiny daughter in a four-hour-per-day nursery school so I could write for four hours five days a week. Those twenty hours without her (twenty-five, counting commute) meant less time with this new child I loved and was just getting to know. I had a major cry at the thought. But ultimately, I bargained with myself that those novel-writing hours for me and school hours for her would be well spent if they gave her the chance to learn different things through other loving adults, and if they gave me time to finish my book and be the writer I needed to be, as well as more energy for my daughter during our mornings before school and afternoons and evenings after. They did; we spent our time together more deliberately than we had when I hadn't been writing. It was a bargain I'm infinitely glad to have made. It was the necessary thing for me to be both writer and parent.

In my own life, waking up a little earlier each day is an easy sacrifice to make in order to write and finish books—the main casualty is that I am charmless by 9:00 p.m. Oh well! But you, dear unique individual, must know your own lexicon of values, and you must bargain accordingly. If you start a social media campaign to market your music, it will cut into the number of quiet hours you have to play. For some people this will be worth it; for others it won't. If you start a twice-weekly gym regimen, it will mean twice a week you cannot linger over breakfast. We must make sacrifices we can live with.

ALIGN INSIDE AND OUT IN OBVIOUS WAYS

It is well-known science that habits are easier to form when the world around us aligns with the internal habit we are trying to master.

Sometimes the necessary thing is so obvious that we feel foolish for ever having not done it. If your relationship needs more sex, an obvious question worth asking is, Are you in bed at the same time, and in good spirits with each other? A whole lot of success in any realm comes down to waking up and going to bed at the right time. The old adage that the amateur studies tactics, the professional studies logistics comes in handy here. You can make any plan you want, but if you don't schedule a time in the day to do it, it simply won't happen. Apply to anything from military success to getting exercise to starting a business. Some low-level, obvious legwork is always involved in order to make something a habit. An act of showing up—again and again.

Sometimes this obvious thing involves leaning into people: If you want to be a fit person, find a gym you like or a group of running buddies. If you want to learn about craft beers and train your palate to be more discerning, then make friends at a brewery. Bring a book to read while you sip and strike up a conversation. Go among the people who do the thing that feels necessary to your growth.

By aligning the inside and out in as many ways as we can, we raise our chances of spending more time doing what we enjoy and less time doing what we don't—in short, that we write our lives in ways that make us happy.

LIFE-EDIT PROMPTS

1. **Write your hierarchy of needs and luxuries.** Draw a triangle with two horizontal lines dividing it. What are your needs, both vital and societal; what are your luxuries? Start at the bottom and work up. In terms of your personal lexicon of luxuries, be truthful, even if it feels ridiculous. Nobody else needs to see. If you had unlimited money, time, and energy, what would you spend it on? What always feels like a good use of resources?

2. **Assess your filter of the necessary.** On the outside of the pyramid you drew in number one lies everything else. Those are not your needs. Those are the things that need not tempt you or draw your attention or make you feel guilty. You can feel free to ignore them, for they are not for you. Keep this list nearby and honor it as much as you do your hierarchy of needs. It is the no-man's-land in terms of your attention—the things that you don't need to invest in at this point of your life (or ever).

3. **Set a reminder.** It may be a simple sticker on your phone, or an alarm, or an association between two things (one of my friends decided that practicing mindfulness was necessary, but she only remembered to do it when she walked up and down the stairs, making every stairstep a walking meditation—and that association has held for her for years). How can you set an easy reminder to yourself to do what is necessary and not do what isn't? For a while my husband and I made and wore green rubber bracelets with *one kind thing* written on the outside, to remind us each day to lead with kindness.

4. **Align inside and out.** Is there a simple, obvious alignment you can make between your inner wish and the outer world? Think basic logistics: Going to bed earlier. Leaving your phone or credit card at home for short spurts of time. Walking instead of driving. Putting the healthy food at the front of the pantry. Smiling at a family member before asking for something. Trying to say yes before no to a child ("Yes, we can go to the park, but it won't be tonight, because now it's bedtime"). What simple small alignment could make a great change?

5. **Shed a pretense.** Is there any place in your life where you continually feel like an imposter? Come up with a way to reframe it—such as saying, "I haven't read much about that—I'd love for you to tell me more." Accept that

this is simply who you are and what you currently know, and that it is your choice to continue gaining knowledge and mastery, or to let it go.

6. **Try a day without.** Try for a single day to go without something that feels necessary by replacing it with something else. For instance, rather than having second helpings when you are already full, have a cup of tea. Rather than flipping through the cable channels when you are bored, what if you spend your downtime doing an activity you say you'd like to do more of (reading, practicing an instrument, calling someone)? Rather than having the last word in an argument when you are upset, on this single day, simply say, "Fair enough" or "We must agree to disagree." Or even "Perhaps you're right." See how it feels to shift your idea of necessary in this way.

7. **Name the bargain.** What would you have to give up if you decided to work toward what feels most necessary in your life? Is it something major, or something negligible? There is always something, however big or small. At most, you might have to move cities or houses; at least, you will have to shift some hours around. If you name your bargain, understand its parameters, and think of what could make such a sacrifice workable or even beneficial, then you are one step closer to accepting the costs of achieving your first-choice life.

PART 2

Edit Your Life

4

EDIT FOR CLARITY

Setting Guardrails with Love

Some of the most poignant daily struggles that I have faced as a young writer-mother are the mornings. If I wanted to live my first-choice life, I needed to get ahead in my books in the first hours of the day, before anyone required my energy for anything else. If I woke before the light to do what nourished me, nothing could upset me. It gave me a full day's immunity to negativity: a shield. By starting my day with writing, exercise, and solitude, I felt impermeable, calm, effective. I felt like my best self.

I would prepare: set my alarm, go to bed early, lay out my clothes—so I could out-wake my children, the earlier the better, and have a quiet two hours to myself to write. But they bested me daily, always in the most loving ways. I'd tiptoe, silent cup of tea in hand, at 5:30 a.m. to my desk—and the huge-diapered, pajama-footed baby would smell me and toddle over, big smile, ready to start the day. I started waking earlier: 5:15, 5:00. There felt something metallic and unkind about pushing back into the fours, but sometimes I did it anyway.

I thought of my ancestors—coal miners and ranchers—and how this was their morning time to push back into the hard, unforgiving rock or to tend to their hungry animals. Hoping this day would not swallow them. I am lucky, immeasurably lucky, to get to do work I choose (writing) in a place (home office) and time (early morning) of my choice. But I could not seem to get up early enough to do my work—my first-choice activity of what makes me feel whole and happy—before the day and its many demands took over. And as Joyce Carol Oates has observed, "The great enemy of writing is being interrupted by other people. Your worst enemy will have your most beloved face."

Focusing on writing before spending the day focused on my household felt like the obvious, necessary guardrail—especially since my husband had a more regular daytime work schedule—but I had to stage some ways to make it work. None worked all the time, though each one worked sometimes; I jostled between them.

One was asking my husband to be on morning duty. He always said yes, but morning duty meant different things to us. I felt it necessary to acknowledge our children at the threshold of their waking and offer some form of love. My husband, on the other hand, felt it necessary to sleep past six, so this whole battle went on during his unconscious hours. If I sent the babies to him, they'd return like boomerangs to me.

The second was the most inspired. It was to set up their own desks in my office, complete with art supplies and snacks, and to try to initiate them to the truth that morning is an excellent time for projects, with its own gravitas and its own treats. We even tried using a timer for "work time." This worked to delight the child and buy me a few minutes at intervals.

The third was to find a coffee shop that opened at 6:00 a.m. This worked every time!

So I bandied among these three, always wrapping by 8:00 a.m. so I could lavish attention on my children for a few minutes before school (my husband took them to school, I picked them up).

And then, to my amazement, the seasons changed and my daughter was no longer my early morning companion—she had learned to sleep past seven—but my son still was. And then suddenly both were sleeping heavy, long nights and no longer desiring to wake early and hang with me. Which, in the dizzy way I remember all things about early parenthood, I found myself missing.

But I have a souvenir from those seven years of trying and failing daily to out-wake my household: I still wake early and write most days before doing anything else. This guardrail enables me to live a full life during the daytime hours—showing up for my kids' school events, collaborating with other artists, teaching a full course load of writing workshops, seeing friends, going for hikes and spontaneous dates with my husband, and tending to the day as it unfolds.

This souvenir ties me forward to my babies—my catalyst for becoming an early-morning writer—and backward to my ancestors, who woke early for their own reasons of survival. I still try to write ahead in my book before anyone speaks my name.

And what is left of our work—if we are lucky, and I mean really lucky—is ourselves.

GUARDRAILS MAKE THE INVISIBLE VISIBLE

Your guardrails stem from your first choices: those absolute-value certainties about who you are, based on close examination of your life.

We all have invisible guardrails: we can find them easily because they protect the tender spots and guard important emotions. When a guardrail is tapped too many times, we get angry or frustrated, because some vital part of us has been threatened. When this happens, it is well worth asking what is on the other side of that guardrail. What does it protect?

On the other side of a guardrail is a cliff you fall down, or a breaking point, or some unsavory consequence. It need not be dire or punitive, but it has to be real. To make an invisible guardrail visible, we need to consider an emotion or situation that we wish to avoid, then set the simplest possible barrier in front of it. Ideally our guardrails prevent us from toppling off this particular cliff into the unpleasantness below. For instance, a writer who wants to avoid losing interest in her project might set the guardrail of touching that project—just for half an hour or so, giving its contents a stir—every weekday. Someone who wants to remain flexible and not lose physical range of motion might set the guardrail of never brushing his teeth until he'd done a little stretching. One of my grandmother's guardrails is that she always made the bed while she was still in it, so that one part of her room would feel orderly when she got out of bed. Guardrails can be big or small, daily or unrelated to time. But they must keep us somehow in line.

The process of making a guardrail visible is both idealistic and practical in nature. It sets the moonshot ideal, and then each day, slowly, *slowly*, it bends the real to meet it. When you set your own guardrails, using love, you state your truths, your comforts, what you can and cannot accept. These guardrails are not bendable by anyone else. No one has the right to argue. Not even—especially not—the people you love most.

This edit asks you to excavate your guardrails or to create them, and to set them out plainly in sight so that everybody can see. This is infinitely preferable to barking out our demands in anger—which is how many of us respond when an invisible guardrail is accidentally bumped.

One of the most important guardrail stories from my own life occurred when I was newly married. I worked all week teaching tenth grade at my old high school, while my new husband worked at home and spent the day alone. On the weekends, after I had spent the week holding out my heart on a plate for my students, I was burnt out of people time ("all peopled out," my sister calls it) and needing solitude. On the weekends, James quite reasonably wanted some time with me, his main person.

What we would do on those early weekends was spend Saturday together, have Sunday brunch with my extended family, hang out some more together, and then around 4:00 p.m. each Sunday we'd get into an argument.

It was like clockwork, and it was always about something dumb. To cool off, I'd go to a café to write in my journal, and then after an hour or two come back home ready to make up and have dinner together.

After a month or so of this, James sensibly asked if we might send me to the café directly after McKetta Brunch, so I could get some Elisabeth-solo, and then when I felt like it I'd come home and we'd spend the rest of the day together.

We tried it—it worked! It was a revelation that something so simple could improve a relationship so much. But what James could see (by looking closely, week after week) is that picking a fight and going off alone after seemed the only way I knew then how to ask for time to myself, and so his suggestion subverted that paradigm.

Now "E-solo" (and J-solo, and anyone-solo) is simply a phrase in our family vocabulary. If you need solo, we remind our kids and our parents and each other, just say so. The beauty of this model is it sets the guardrail in plain sight and collectively respects it. Nobody gets mad or should get mad when anyone states, "I need some solo right now." We all are entitled by the culture of our family to stake out our own space and time. I once heard Cora as a baby explain to the dog, "My need pace!" (space).

Everyone has guardrails internally—boundaries, must-haves, personal rules of the road. The trick with this edit is making them visible so they don't cause hidden emotional ruckuses when tapped.

GUARDRAILS MUST HAVE LOGIC

A guardrail is not arbitrary but stems from the very real facts of your life's who/what/when/where. A guardrail is useful because you know when you've hit it—and you can self-correct before falling off the cliff entirely and crashing at the bottom.

When we edited our life by moving to the Shed, we set a short list of basic daily and weekly guardrails that would respect the small square footage and allow us to peacefully coexist. If the guardrail is that all our clothes must fit into two small bins and a hook with eight hangers, there must be a logical reason why (in our case, because that's all the space we have for clothes).

Sometimes the reason is less visible but equally logical. Like the law, a guardrail comes into existence when something goes wrong for the guardrail's not having been there. When my husband first fried an egg in the Shed and the smell lingered for days in everybody's bedroom, we decided that a plant-based kitchen would be a good idea in this particular dwelling.

Food guardrails are a good place to start because they are so clear. Mark Bittman, celebrated food journalist and cookbook author, set himself a guardrail after his doctor expressed worry about his blood pressure: He decided to eat vegan before 6:00 p.m. (VB6, he calls it). This means he can continue to sample the great foods of the world for his evening meal, while following doctor's orders for the rest of the day.

Sometimes good guardrails solve problems by twos. My husband devised a clever guardrail that helped our children both become more capable and work together more: Whenever they whined about doing some small achievable thing that felt difficult—such as making their bed or cleaning the shower—he'd assign them the task of working together on it. They learned through this guardrail to ask each other before they asked us—for when they whined at us, we would consistently send them back to help each other. It is worth considering if there are any challenges in your life that can be solved "by twos"—as this guardrail solved the twin challenges for us of children giving up too easily on ordinary tasks and bickering with each other while doing so. It should be a logical win-win.

Guardrails should not be too restrictive. You can hit them and bump off. But you try not to hit them. The point is to live comfortably within them, to safely stay on the road, and not have to think about them too much.

Here are ours during this era:

- **Clothes:** We would pay $1 a pound to drop off our laundry each Friday at the wash-and-fold, as we'd have no washer or dryer. We four would share two towels and teach the kids how to hang them. We would keep seasonal wardrobes of eight outfits each to last us between laundry days. We'd store our off-season clothes in a bin in the garage.

- **Toys:** We would keep the kids' toys in a bin in the garage and let them choose a few for their smaller toy boxes that fit on the Shed shelves. The kids could swap out toys anytime. We'd engage them in a yearly spring clean with the option of donating old toys to smaller children.

- **Work:** We would do our work in a shared office outside the house two blocks away (a converted garage space) and build a tiny 3' × 5' "emergency office" inside the Shed.

- **Child duty:** We would share child-rearing responsibility equally: my husband would be on morning duty while I worked, I'd be on afternoon duty while he worked, we'd try to have dinner and breakfast as a family as often as possible, and we'd take turns with evening duty.

- **Money:** We would live on half our combined income and place the other half directly into a savings account for investment and travel (in just proportions). We'd limit ourselves to a cash budget for food, the area where we are likeliest to overspend.

- **Fairness:** We would put the children "in the same boat" so they'd help each other; when they misbehaved, we'd ask them to help develop a system and a consequence to "get to good." We would try to be fair. On odd days our daughter would get first choice of things, on even days our son.

- **Dates:** My husband and I would have dates every Tuesday (the only night our babysitter was free). We'd take turns having weekend dates with each child. Less fun but equally necessary, we'd have a weekly financial meeting to quarantine household business conversations.

- **Rest:** We would try to get the kids into bed most nights by eight. On weekends or holidays, we would all take a midday siesta. Cardinal rule: No talking about sensitive subjects after 9:00 p.m.

- **Friends:** We love hosting, so we would keep a sofa that could convert to a guest bed and invite kids' friends to bring sleeping bags for sleepovers. In the warm months, we'd host dinners outside. In the freezing months, we'd host smaller dinners inside or bring meals over to friends' houses.

- **Food:** We would keep a vegan kitchen for ease, cleanliness, and to maximize space; we'd have no dishwasher, a mini-fridge, and pantry space enough for about twenty glass jars of beans, grains, nuts, and healthy snacks. We would not keep food in the Shed that we didn't want ourselves and our kids to eat.

- **Cleaning:** We would leave time to clean and tidy as we go and teach the kids to do so too—for while a tiny house cleans up fast, one person's mess renders it unusable for everyone else. Saturday we would enlist the kids in a bigger house-clean, which would take a few hours.

- **Travel:** We would live in the Shed in the fall and the spring, when Boise weather is lovely and the kids are in school, and we would consolidate our traveling into the (three-week) winter and (three-month) summer breaks. We'd plan for a full year or two abroad when the kids got older.

- **Community:** We would get memberships to all the local places that are fun for kids—discovery center, zoo, botanical garden, library, swimming pool—and we would do outings after school most days.

Each one of these is logical and has a real consequence if we break it. In the Shed, if the art supplies do not fit into the art box, they must go out of the house; we break the art box if we try to fight this guardrail. We only have one table, so we cannot have dinner unless we tidy as we go; we get glitter and glue in our food if we fight this guardrail. If both parents do not cook, we will overspend on eating out, or we will have too many scavenge-meals (the latter not such a bad thing, really). If we come home straight from school for days on end rather than having some sort of afternoon outing to "get our crazies out," as Cora calls it, we all usually get stir-crazy by dinner. If James and I embark on an argument after bedtime, we both wake up feeling sad and disconnected. We've hit all of these consequences and seen the results—some worse than others.

Keeping only food we wish to eat in the house saves us a whole lot of saying no. Scott likes to make smoothies, which he has full license to do—barring tomatoes and cumin, there's not much that we keep in the Shed that can ruin it (I list those two from experience—we threw that smoothie away!). He knows the general recipe and where the ingredients are kept. Whatever he makes, it can pretty much only be good. This is a guardrail that empowers him, and it gives the rest of us a good breakfast.

A further guardrail that the Shed required us to make involved cleaning chemicals. There is about a foot of under-sink storage, so the only cleaning supplies we keep and use are vinegar and castile soap. This means that the kids can rummage around in the under-sink cabinet all day and find nothing that will harm them.

And if we want to have lunch, we must wash our breakfast dishes, because we keep a tight ship's kitchen and only have eight of what we need: eight plates, eight mugs, eight bowls, eight knives, eight spoons, eight forks. Enough for us and four guests. Such a life requires that we take a short pause, clear the table, do the washing before we move on to anything else.

In an edited house, this order comes naturally: every activity, every "work" has a stage of preparation, a stage of the act itself, and a stage of cleaning up. Without such guardrails, we have to make constant unimportant decisions. Without such guardrails, we live in all three stages at once, which to me in the big house always felt like one stage: a frenzied, endless cleaning up. Without guardrails at home, housework swallows up hours. Once upon a time, before we edited our lives, when the kids asked me to read to them—something I love to do—I would usually be in the middle of some endless project (dishes, laundry, tidying). So I'd answer, "When I am finished," thinking I could relax into reading once the housework was done. It never was.

Guardrails prevent the unimportant things in your life from overflowing and drowning out the important ones.

ASK DIRECTLY FIRST

Once you have spent time thinking about these first few edits, you will likely have a sense of your first choice for an ideal life and the guardrails needed to protect it. In order to have a guardrail seen and respected, we need to articulate it to others.

This often means asking directly first. When you ask directly, you invite someone else to consider their guardrails. What are they comfortable doing, giving, or receiving? Try to ask directly for it to those who can help you attain it. Ask your parents to please respect your life choices, your children to please make their own lunches, and your boss to give you more responsibility and a raise. Waiting for others to guess what we want (or trying to guess what others want, without asking) is exhausting, and about as accurate as looking into a crystal ball.

These days I try to practice without fear the art of Kindly Asking Strangers—such as when staying in a hotel when the neighbor is making noise at 2:00 a.m. It is tempting to simply call the front desk, but kinder and braver is to make the direct request, while appealing to their higher selves: "Hi, guys, will you please keep it down? We're all asleep next door." It might work, it might not, but it combines (1) the specific direct ask with (2) the relatable reason behind it, and most people will respond reasonably.

Speaking up and other forms of self-assertion have not come naturally to me. For much of my life, I felt, instinctively, that politeness mattered more than honesty; it took me a long time to learn to say exactly what I meant (case in point: E-solo story earlier!). In truth, both politeness and honesty matter—and can easily coexist. In truth, we never really know the universe inside another person, the intricate constellations of how and what they feel. By asking directly, both on behalf of our own first choices and in a true effort to understand or advocate for another person's, we lay aside the guesswork and simply try. This counts for a lot. It opens a bottleneck that for many people lasts a lifetime. One couple I know, with forty years of solid marriage behind them, required three sessions with a marriage counselor before she could ask him not to use her computer without her permission. It is always funny what becomes a taboo in a given setting or relationship—it is simply what we are afraid to ask, because of what we indirectly suspect to be true.

When we are in the habit of asking directly, taboos vanish at once. Many people are afraid to say their true thoughts, for they

believe the truth is not welcome. But it takes many more steps—
and wastes infinitely more energy—to dance around the truth
than to step on someone's foot, and apologize. Truth is always
the first choice, even if it has
many faces. Even if our truths

**Truth is always the
first choice.**

conflict, it is better to talk about
them and to listen with an open
mind. Asking directly is a form of
telling the truth.

Directness is equally as important in the realm of work as it is
in the realm of love. At times, in a job, we are not given raises or
more interesting work simply because we never asked for it. At
times, in a relationship, when we feel annoyed about something, it
is because love is being offered to us in a way we don't see, or we
are giving love in a way that is not being seen. A simple direct ask
can solve this.

In my early years of marriage, I used to try to anticipate my
husband's needs and try to solve them. My efforts always resulted
in annoying him for they made him feel that I felt he was incom-
petent. Also, in the early days of my marriage, he offered me frequent criticism of how I could improve things I felt I did well
enough, such as feeding the dogs and driving. This annoyed me
and hurt my feelings. We both went on like this, until a direct conversation enlightened us: I saw that he intended his criticism of me
as a gift to help me do things more efficiently—he meant it well;
and he saw that I have my own way of doing things, and that his

words were causing me stress—and we developed a system for how he could offer feedback without frustrating me, and how he could know when to say nothing and just accept that my way of feeding the dog or driving the car is different from his. He saw too that my daily efforts to do various tasks (imperfectly) for him were my way of showing love—and he acknowledged his annoyance and pointed out that he is a grown-up and doesn't need me to meet all his needs. He suggested other ways he would appreciate for me to show love. An effective direct conversation lightened the load for us both.

Now I do the same things for my children, parents, friends, and students. Rather than guessing, I simply ask: "Would you like me to make you kids lunch, or would you prefer to scavenge?" (Usually scavenge.) As long as I am happy with either answer, it is a fair and useful question. Or for friends who are visiting town: "Would you like for us to plan out the days of your visit, or leave them open and spontaneous?" (Usually open—which saves me time of planning something that nobody actually wants to do.) Or for students: "Would you like to try to solve this book problem together, or would you rather keep writing and see what happens?" These are all different ways of asking the same question: Through which avenue do you wish to receive what I wish to give?

We ask directly both for people to share their needs and for them to help us in meeting our own.

With the people we live with and love most, sometimes we have to ask directly first—and second—and third—every day. I lose my patience with my children around the third ask when I wish for them to do a simple task, such as clearing their dishes or brushing their teeth (morning routines go a long way in helping me stay patient). When I can feel the possibility of "losing the plot," as my friend Asti calls it, I say to the children: "I have now asked you directly three times to . . ." Usually that wakes them into attention. It is an I-statement. It is true. It contains a specific number. It is an acknowledgment that I am doing my best. I am asking directly. From a very young age, children can understand this concept. So can most reasonable people.

I can also ask myself directly if I am rebelling against some system that I have made for myself that I simply don't want to do. Can I postpone doing my grading to this afternoon, if what I really want to do this morning is go for a walk? Can I say no to attending this late-night dance performance—even though I love the friend who invited me—simply because I don't like to stay up late? Can I see her for lunch another day, or ask if we might see the matinee instead? If I am dreading something or feeling anxious about it, even a small thing, it is worth stopping to ask myself directly why. We can allow ourselves grace.

The simplest direct ask to relieve ourselves of something that feels a burden is the question "Do I have to?" My kids ask this one a lot. It is an important question. Often the answer is no. Or "not now." I have asked other people this question in many forms. "How important is it that I . . . ?" or "Is there someone else who would enjoy . . . ?" Or in the positive: "How specifically can I be of most use?" or "What can I do *today* for you?" These are all good questions that invite others to state their needs directly.

You can also ask directly for a better way to contribute and be helpful—for example, when I was invited to volunteer at my kids' school, not wanting to be assigned a dull task, I asked directly for the opportunity to tell fairy tales (my first-choice volunteer idea) to the children's classes every week. The school accepted with delight. Asking directly is a form of telling the truth. Truth is always the first and simplest choice, even if it has many faces. Asking directly first is a way of culling second-choice behavior from cluttering relationships—including the relationship with self.

GUARDRAILS HAVE SEASONS

The guardrails you set during calm times will require reevaluation during crises—though best not to abandon them in crisis, as they may keep you sane as you pick up the pieces.

Several of our guardrails vanished during the pandemic: taking regular outings after school, school in general, clear bedtimes, cash budget for groceries. We found that even our guardrails triaged themselves, leaving only the most essential (no sensitive subjects after 9:00 p.m. always ends up at the top of the list, as does trying to put the kids in the same boat). As Eisenhower put it: "Plans are useless, but planning is everything." Guardrails align us internally, so that when our lives get edited by external forces, we can still hold true to something.

The guardrails set during the school year will be different from the ones that make sense in summer. Before virustime, and I hope again one day, I had a tradition of taking the children each year to Boston, where I teach summer school. My husband stays home, for summer is his busiest work season. During those one to two months, I am a solo parent—though I always meet either my mom or our wonderful babysitter so there can be two adults. In the day, we explore the city, and at night, I teach. We have three summertime guardrails that stay constant from year to year, framing our daily landscape.

One, we go out of the house after breakfast. The logic: We have traveled far to live differently from how we live at home. We cannot spend all summer inside playing with Lego sets (though often we spend a hot afternoon this way). Whether to the post office or to the museum or to the park doesn't matter. We go.

Two, we take a two-hour rest after lunch. The logic: the kids need a break, and I need to grade.

Three, when we eat out, the children have "autonomy" (their favorite word) as long as they (mostly) balance their own meals according to the Harvard food plate: half fruits and vegetables, a quarter protein, a quarter grain. The logic: it is science, and the last thing I want is to spend all summer playing food police.

Each day that we respect these rules, they grow firmer in the soil of our lives. Eventually, they do not budge.

YOUR GUARDRAILS ARE YOUR RESPONSIBILITY

I keep my personal guardrails written on my desk and revisit them each season or so. The details change, but the big picture holds: My guardrails serve as a bare beautiful minimum for how I want to live, and they are reflected in my daily, weekly, and seasonal rituals. They are my personal practice, my life recipe for doing today's work today (writing first, and grading student papers within a day of receiving them, not making social plans before noon), exercising simply (mostly walks, yoga, various embarrassing exercises with a resistance band), spending time with loved ones each day (including calling or seeing a friend most afternoons, doing my best to listen without interrupting or advising, finding a way to do one kind thing for a stranger), and trying to learn something each day and do something fun.

If I don't uphold these guardrails, nobody will. If a friend wants to talk before noon, it is my responsibility to myself to say, "I'll call you after lunch." Or better yet, work until noon with my phone on silent, except for a few emergency callers (like my husband and kids and parents) who can call through. If I fail to uphold my personal guardrails, I will be worrying about work when I'm with my kids, or regretting my parenting failures when I am working. Not a first-choice use of time.

Some people have the tendency to fight guardrails set by anyone, especially loved ones. Around these people, no matter how much we love them, we must wear our guardrails like armor. In the instances when a family member persists in fighting them, the loving thing is to ask directly why. Ask those people what exactly this guardrail means to them, and why it seems to pose a threat. The geometry of spousal guardrails is different from what we'd need to set with our children or with our parents or friends. I try to hold them all with love. I fail. I try again.

Even without fights, it can still feel hard to manage good guardrails. Setting and upholding them can wear a person out. Willpower, much science suggests, is a muscle that tires out, so it's wise to conserve it for when we need it. One thing I love about living in a very small house is that the house itself sets many guardrails, so that I don't have to. The house plays bad cop so that we grown-ups can consistently play good cop.

The more edited our life is, the more transparent the guardrails must be. The more people we live with (each with their own guardrails), the more relaxed we must be about everything except for our guardrails. One of my swimmer husband's guardrails is that he must get into the water at least twice a week. If he doesn't, he feels grumpy and landlocked. My children are beginning to develop their own; I watch closely to learn them and try to respect them.

When I feel tempted to ignore my own guardrails, it helps to remember their obvious logic and reason for being: If I have to manage my children during their chores, that means I do not do my own chores, and so everything takes longer and we won't have time to do our fun Saturday night ritual of pizza and a family movie. If I bring up household business on date night with James, it turns connection time into transaction time, and we can feel the loss all week. There is a clear (but not dire) consequence if we fail. Therefore, we learn week by week to succeed.

When a system fails, as they all will on certain days, return to it again the next day. And the next day. If it's a good system, it will work and eventually become a habit. If it doesn't work for a month, reevaluate. It is always easier to follow a system that you've set than to fight and reinvent it.

When two systems clash, as they all will on certain days, then you must triage. Say you have one guardrail of doing a "no tech day" on Saturdays, and another guardrail that you keep your phone on for your child. Pick the higher-stakes one. The worst that can happen with the first is that you may feel a bit fried tomorrow for having not truly relaxed today, but the worst that can happen with the second is that your child will really need you and you won't be there to help. Pick the vital one. There will be time for the other, but maybe not today.

Living an edited life requires making time in the present moment to do the necessary thing. Not spending today dealing with yesterday's work. Much energy is freed by setting good guardrails with love, then trusting and upholding them. Guardrails protect what matters most—for your own soul's survival.

LIFE-EDIT PROMPTS

1. **Turn the invisible visible.** Look in your life for the moments you misbehave or get angry. Could this anger be a sign that an invisible guardrail has been tapped too hard or too often? Over the course of a week, look for and list out these tender spots in your life—welcome them as your invisible guardrails that protect your basic needs. What would they look like as guardrails set in plain sight?

2. **Pick a "guardrail guru."** A good way to discern good guardrails is to observe any people in your life who make clear what they need, relieving you of the need to read their minds. If they have to leave at a certain time, they will tell you. You never have to worry that they will do something against their will out of guilt or politeness, or something they will regret later. Pick a "guardrail guru" in your life—someone who has excellent guardrails and seems to wear them easily—and observe this person in action. How do they make guardrails clear in a way that feels respectful to others? In this exercise, you might find examples of people who have good guardrails—say a boss at work who is clear with expectations—but who do not communicate these expectations in a morale-raising way. Could the

same effect be achieved more gently and kindly, while remaining as clear? How might you do this in your own life?

3. **Observe guardrails in the world.** Literal ones that keep your car from driving off a cliff on a curved road; a dog that gives a short, nonaggressive warning bark; a restaurant that closes at a clear time so their employees can go home. Notice how guardrails protect something, and get into the habit of seeing this as a positive and respectful thing, not a negative and inconvenient one.

4. **Say no to say yes.** This is one of the daily mantras of my wise friend Cathy. She observes that everything she says yes to means that she says no to something else. If we accept that our life is made up of yeses and nos, look for some of the nos you can say that would lead way to greater, most bountiful yeses. For example, by saying no to staying up late to watch television, what would you be able to wake early and say yes to in the morning?

5. **Say yes to say no.** The wise converse. Are there any things you can let go of by simply saying yes? By agreeing to a small request today—for example, doing fifteen minutes of extra work to clean up a problem that has arisen, or helping a colleague understand something, or giving your full attention to someone now

so they won't later try to get your attention in negative, less productive ways—can you remove future obstacles? In *Getting Things Done*, David Allen has the "two-minute rule" for things that are more sensible to do now. Works wonders.

6. **Ask directly for exactly what you need.** Write several versions of a question (to a family member, colleague, boss, imaginary person living or dead) that requests something that feels vital to your emotional survival—then distill to the way that is the shortest, the clearest, the kindest. Can you say it in under a paragraph? How about a single sentence? Write a second question as a backup in case the first ask fails, some version of: "I have now asked you directly three times to X. Is there another way you suggest I try?"

5

EDIT FOR GROWTH

Respecting the Seasons

How we edit is how we live. My son was cleaning out his camera, for it was too full for him to take any more photos. He asked for my help. The first photo was of a dead fly.

"Keep or delete?" I asked.

"Keep," he said with certainty.

The next twenty-eight photos were fuzzy shots of family. He instructed me to delete all those.

How we edit is how we live.

The emotional souvenir I took away from being his sous photographer: Scott sees enough of us these days, but a close-up of a dead fly for a young nature guy is magic.

I would've edited differently. But it's his camera, his fly, his life, and he must edit as he is now. I must edit as I am now.

GROWTH IS NECESSARY: THE BRAVE THING

No matter what life you live, some growth out of your comfort zone is necessary in order not to atrophy mentally and physically. We all have versions of ourselves that we wish to stretch to be: braver, kinder, smarter, calmer, healthier, wiser, more creative, more fun. We may never be these people to the full extent of our imaginings. But stretching toward these expanded versions of self can and will happen with practice. If I want to be a more adventurous person, I need to initiate more adventures in my life. Simple as that. If I want to be a better map reader, I should spend more time navigating.

What is the thing out of your comfort zone—the brave thing—that you can try to do?

One person's brave thing may feel easy to you—or it may feel impossible. Adjust for who you are and where you wish to grow. In the words of Oscar Wilde: "Be yourself. Everyone else is already taken." Better to follow your own version of brave than someone else's. There are certain hard boundaries for all of us, things we can and cannot do. It is worth asking: What is the direction of your "brave thing"—and what challenges for yourself (small or large) could be necessary to reach for?

My husband and I tell our children to do one brave thing a day. Sometimes it is physically brave—jumping into the water, suiting up for a run in the rain. Sometimes it is emotionally brave: speaking publicly or participating in a difficult conversation. I try to do this myself too; I am not naturally brave, but I try to stretch myself as a habit, as early as possible in the day. I imagine there is a Morning Courage Club of people worldwide waking up to face their fears and go into the day feeling braver for it, and I try to join it as often as I can.

Emotional courage comes more easily to me than physical courage. If I make a fool of myself, so what! But physical courage has an injury risk I'm not all that comfortable with. Most of my bravest things, then, fall along emotional lines, such as telling a story onstage, or showing my vulnerability, whereas my husband's brave tends to be physical (big swims, big kayaks, big athletic feats in general). We are all wise to try to do brave things in both realms, to the extent of our abilities and our feelings about risk and growth.

How to know in which direction to grow? Look at your moonshot and close-read your feelings about it. What feelings have driven you in life thus far: longing for security, success, love? Such questions will help determine your answer.

Also, there are eras for growth and eras for rest and replenishment: those latter ones we must tend like a garden. We must not force ourselves to grow too soon. Courage is admirable but not when forced.

Where I live in Idaho, everybody seems to love camping, mountain biking, and any number of outdoor pleasures—and I showed up there at age thirty, an indoor girl who likes to read and write and go see plays. But I wanted to join the camping throngs. My husband and my dear friend Emerald, experienced backpackers both, made me a plan for growth: I would drive five hours to meet Emerald and we'd sleep in the woods for two days. It was so brave! I was so afraid! Even the drive was outside my comfort zone, for much of it was not even in cell service range. I realized during the drive that I did not have a map and did not remember how to change a tire, which made me feel vulnerable and, frankly, stupid. But I bought a map. And I reminded myself that I had always been able to count on the kindness of strangers, and that I had changed a tire before and that the tires on the car were new. And the nights in the woods, though not something I'd do again immediately, left me feeling refreshed and braver, and willing to go again.

Bravery brings with it a paradox: it is necessary to challenge ourselves in small and big ways; also, sometimes a challenge can go too far. Like anything, there is the balance. A good teacher—whether a swimming coach or a piano tutor—can help us sensibly expand what we can do. When I do a brave thing, I always feel exhausted afterward, and one psychic inch bigger.

THE SPIRIT OF THE THING

There are seasons for everything, and we must grow into them. You are not the same person you were at the beginning of last year. Your children are not the same children. Your mother is a different mother. In subtle ways, your mate is a different mate. The book I write today I could not have written a year ago. Or a year from now. So what continues, then? What of your life lasts from year to year, the hard seed in the thrashing water?

When we edit for seasons, we must look for the spirit of the thing that transcends. Sometimes it gets lost. If you are a doctor who wishes to shift into a new season of practicing medicine, it is useful to consider which parts of medicine give you the most energy: The research? Seeing the patients? Learning from colleagues you admire? Simply being in the office and trusting your expertise? Conversely, which part depletes you? Turn into the next season with your eye on preserving the part that feeds your soul. You can build around it. As a writer, I had to ask myself this question when determining which sorts of projects I'd take on: Would it be journalism? Advertising? Legal briefs? I considered all of these. But what ultimately makes writing alive for me is the magical ability of words to carry feelings and connect people—that and the layers of meaning and wisdom that a sentence can contain. Therefore, I would write to try to heal and teach and connect. This would lead me toward poetry, creative writing, philosophy, and teaching. These, to me, felt like the eternal things.

What are your eternal things?

Whatever choices you make for work and love, ask regularly whether they are worthy of your heart and brain and hands. This simple question will carry you through all seasons. Do your days use every bit of you? We should strive for it to be so. Like a house where there is no wasted space, an edited life has no unexcavated corners and very little wasted energy—every piece serves several purposes, and nothing sits around, season after season, unused.

An edited life reminds us to live seasonally. In an edited home, it is necessary to have seasonal closets, changed at the year's junctures. I like this. I like putting away our flip-flops, floppy sun hats, and Razor scooters at summer's end—knowing I will pull them out of their garage storage bin again when it gets warm. There is no space in the Shed for all the objects required for all the lives we might live, but only room for the objects and ambitions for this life, right now.

Living seasonally means we get to say goodbye to certain things while welcoming others. It gives a predictable cycle, following the earth's cycle.

> **An edited life reminds us to live seasonally.**

The Shed feels full in winter, insulated with our puffer jackets and hot-water bottles and my sunlamp; then it lightens in April when we wash our heavy sweaters, hats, gloves, the kids' little fleece infinity scarves, and our puffer coats, and roll them into their bin, knowing there are summer days ahead. In April we also bring inside the snow-cone maker from its bin of "overflow appliances."

Even if we *do* have space for each season in our dwelling and in our schedule, it benefits us to think more broadly about seasons in our lives. For even a single day has its own sections or seasons, albeit lasting only a few hours. My day moves through the spring of the writing morning; the summer of a day spent enjoying my children, spouse, and friends; the autumn-feeling evening hours of teaching and exchanging wisdom with my students; and the silent winter of sleep. These seasons are predictable: By not trying to do one season's work in another season, I can meet each one with my whole heart. By making sure that I give my full attention to each season, I do not spend the others worrying about what seasons will come and what seasons have passed.

SEASONS AND PAYING ATTENTION

Our entire lives can be divided into seasons. If we are lucky, our childhood is steeped in learning and play; our adolescence a time of considering possible futures and specializing our interests; our twenties trying out those futures that most interest us, which sometimes feels as haphazard and luck-driven as simply throwing darts at different targets to see what hits. My thirties have been for producing—babies and books—and here I stand after forty, wondering at it all.

Wisdom means knowing deep-seated certainties about oneself, while having to be flexible in external ways. Getting wiser, then, means being willing to change our position—again and again—in response to the external world. This must be why the great wisdoms always feel so distilled, as small as seeds. They must be so in order to survive—to last the seasons of sickness and health, youth and age, work and leisure, confidence and crisis. They must take root in whichever soil we stand on in our life's journey.

I think too of the future seasons when my children take my place. Will I have edited my life so as not to leave a mess for them? Certain cultures honor a ritual called a death clean, whose name gives me chills even as I write it. But I recognize this need. In shedding what we do not need for this season, we honor our future selves and the others who will have to clean up after us; we have done the editing now, while we are fit in body and mind. We have not demanded other people's time to steward things that are our own responsibility. By modeling this act for our children, we hope they will confidently find their own lives' shape, their own distilled wisdoms and seeds. Such seeds will last; they will reseed, adding to the green in the seasons that come after we are gone. In this way, the small act of editing as a habit becomes a paid-forward gift, a lifesaver, an act of great respect.

Sometimes, between seasons, it takes time to get started. There is no such thing as a summer routine; there is only, in my experience, happy chaos. Routine exists when school starts, both mine and the kids'. In autumn, after two months of living away from home, we settle back into the routine for work and school. The sand that we have joyously flung up all summer is beginning to fall through the water, and settle. We clean house. We switch our summer clothes for fall clothes. The children need new socks and underwear; we are all out of loose tea. We buy things. We call it replacing, for in such a house we cannot accumulate. Though as I settle into my own work rhythm—the new students, this year's books—I find myself drifting into thoughts of the hausfrau. I forgive these thoughts—it is autumn, after all. *Write*, I tell myself. *Spend three or four hours inside the book.* I acquiesce for one hour, then spend two hours ordering a bounty of tea online. Oh, irony! I am supposed to be writing about minimalism. As the days shorten, I will deepen and settle too. I will root down and refocus. I will find in me a thousand words to write—and then I will break midmorning, make soup, walk with the dog into the mountains.

There are seasons of place as there are seasons of time. And in both, sometimes we must uproot for fun, other times to save our lives. Changing season can be joyful or terrible, depending on the context. But if we are living a well-edited life, we can meet each season to the best of our abilities.

This morning is a rainy morning. My son woke early and is cuddled under our single throw blanket that he calls "fuzzy fuzzy." This morning, I think, as I see the rain and think of the seasons when we are required by weather to move inside, how quickly the season of childhood sloughs off, like any delicate skin. The more I think of seasons, the more I think of how regularly we all must shed.

There are seasons and they spin fast. We must constantly edit out those things that keep us from paying attention.

VOLUNTARY LOSS: SEASON, REASON, OR LIFE

The seasons train us four times a year, depending on where we live, to move on. They prepare us for two types of loss: voluntary loss and involuntary loss.

One of my friends from a beautiful short season when I lived in California nearly two decades ago told me, "There are friends for season, reason, and life." She was a dear friend for a season, then our lives went different ways. Her souvenir from our friendship is that she moved with me to Austin, where she now has the best life she can imagine. My souvenir, among other things, is this seed of her wisdom, of acceptance that even if something is not forever, it can still be of great value, something that impacts our lives for the better.

I keep my friends a long time. I plan to keep my husband forever. I feel close with my family. The people I have are very likely the people I'm going to have. My work, then, is to tend and nurture them, to enjoy them and give them my attention—and to make room to keep others for a season, and then others for a new season, making way for the possibility of life, or not. To pay attention to them now, as they are. It is worthwhile for us all to consider our relationships in this context: Where do yours fit, and are you happy with that?

In the Shed, we have dog seasons and dogless seasons. Because we like to travel in the winter and summer, we keep the dog in the fall and spring, when we have an ordinary schedule due to the kids' school calendar. In the traveling seasons, Posy the Labrador goes to her other family, who are delighted to see her.

This is our last single day, this season, with our dog. I will miss her. I am ready for her to go. Being an adult means holding two contrasting ideas in one's head at the same time, and believing both to be true. The children are proud of her: She is being trained by her other family to be a therapy dog, a job she seems born to do. Therefore, she will spend more time there this year than with us. Today I skip the library to be home with her, to enjoy this last day of Labrador season. Outside the trees are perfectly still—I look hard and cannot see a wind. The clouds keep still too. If it weren't for an occasional squirrel bolting along the wooden fence, I could be tricked into believing that the entire scene outside my window was done in paint.

What we learn in the Shed is that season, reason, and life are all valid and can leave an equally valuable imprint on a life.

BE KIND TO YOUR COMMITTEE OF SELVES

It is tempting to look back on our earlier seasons' selves and snort at their shortcomings. How much she didn't know! Look who he was dating! How embarrassing. All the cringey things.

But as my older friends constantly remind me, all those selves are still inside us—the shy, bookish nine-year-old, the party-girl nineteen-year-old, the thirty-six-year-old fresh from chrysalis, the fifty-one-year-old who reevaluated everything, the seventy-one-year-old who at last learned to play the mandolin—and all the way up, if we are lucky. In short, we all house a veritable committee of selves, former, present, and future. Don't believe your life with its today-knowledge is superior. With any luck, you are happier and more accepting of yourself. But you cannot say ever that the earlier eras didn't teach you something.

Forgetting this was a bad habit I sometimes fell into when we first moved into the Shed. I'd say things like, "I'm so glad we're not in the big house anymore!" Then I'd see my children's faces fall. For as much as they were willing to go with me into this adventure of minimalism, they loved the big house. It was where their childhoods played out. They experienced real happiness there, and so did I. Even if we stepped somewhere else after it, in pursuit of more and different happiness.

Speak with respect of your earlier selves. Remember the details lovingly. My writing teacher used to say "she" when talking about her much younger self. It was strange to me at first, but then I saw its logic. She could speak of that young woman with awe and respect and humor. Now she was an ancient in her nineties who looked nothing like the girl who wrote her first books. Don't throw the baby out with the bathwater. Remember it all, or as much as you can, in all the beauty you can recall.

There is something in every era that is alive. Locate it. Shape around it. There is something in each era worth remembering and preserving. Look for it in each era, and specifically in this era. In a beautiful essay about keeping a notebook, Joan Didion wrote that it helps her keep in touch with her earlier selves. This sort of alignment contributes to the vital feeling of self-respect (the topic of yet another terrific Didion essay!). In my lexicon of values, I believe these all relate to the alignment of inner/outer: our outer life reflects who we know ourselves internally to be.

So much mythology and psychology divides the life into three selves: the young (growing) self, who is defined by being the son or daughter; the middle-aged (grown) self, who may be mother or father, creator or entrepreneur or worker or community leader; the elderly self, who has a wise life perspective while facing his or her death. It is worth considering and anticipating these seasons with love and acceptance in ourselves and others.

THE THRILL OF VARIETY

The limitations or conditions of one era will give way to the facts of the next. It is like a game of Goldilocks. Too small, too big, just right. But "just right" will not last forever. "Too big" teaches us one thing. "Too small" teaches us another. Springs of working hard feel as if they should be followed by lazy, meandering summers. Courting opposites both teaches us and balances us. Learning to live a full life is never a waste of time. It counts toward the person we are becoming.

Each era has the potential to offer something new and instructive and good. I had a professor who once said, "You cannot control how long your life will be, but you can fill it with as many experiences and stories as possible to make it good and fat!" Or as the 1920s Jazz Age icon Zelda Fitzgerald put it, "The only emotion which cannot be replicated is the thrill of variety."

It feels lovely both to do a certain thing every day and to change our habits and lives. I think we can do both when we think of life in seasons and of ourselves as being growth minded. For that's all that most lives amount to: a repeated series of actions—reading, running, parenting, cooking, writing, raking, fishing, arguing in court—that you look back and remember with fondness.

Once I wanted to see more of a friend, and I wanted to do more yoga. My friend and I decided to do a lovely winter streak of meeting for her lunch hour on Wednesdays to do online yoga classes—followed by splitting a giant burrito! Then the season ended—but it bonded us and was fun. Season, reason, life. Sometimes a friend for life is kept by the investment of a season. For a season of two years, I brought weekly soup to a neighbor. She was finding it hard to find time to cook, and I was finding that I was throwing away excess soup that my family was sick of eating.

My Poetry for Strangers project was a streak that brought variety to my days as a brand-new mother. I had felt that I wanted to get better at writing poems, and I wanted to spend more time on adventures outside the house with my children. This seven-year streak combined these two wishes in the loveliest of ways, for once a week, when my children and I met an interesting stranger, I'd ask him or her for a word to use in a poem and for an email address to share the poem. During this season, I made some poet friends; got some poems published; learned to trust my writing discipline; modeled for my children the truth that if you offer kindness to strangers, they will very likely show you kindness back; and came out of it feeling like a true poet. So many valuable emotional souvenirs! When the pandemic hit and it was no longer easy to meet strangers in the course of the day, I let this streak come to an end. I had loved it—but the season turned, and I felt in my heart it had been enough.

RESET BUTTONS AND LAYERING ACTIVITIES

A further benefit of living with an eye to the seasons is that there are naturally occurring reset buttons—times when you are required to stop while you're ahead. It is good to have a daily, weekly, monthly, and yearly reset. So we work up to the reset button, trusting that rest will come.

For a day, that is night. For a week, that is the weekend. In medieval society, as hard as the serfs worked, there were well over a hundred "holy days" or holidays.

I like to have a week each season for rebooting—rethinking projects—reorganizing my bins (both metaphorical and physical) from summer to fall or fall to winter. I also take a yearly reset button each summer. Summer I am free, light-handed, ready to build life back up again in the fall in any way I choose. I tend to build it mostly the same way: same schedule, same or similar classes, same friends seen on the same basis. But I have a reset time to make sure I go into these commitments deliberately. If I am in a writing group that meets monthly, my last meeting will be in May. If during June, July, August, I miss it, then I can rejoin come September. Each fall, the children re-choose their activities—the sport and the art they will practice that school year—or we choose anew for them.

In order to go all in on anything, we need to know both that it will go on in the long run (some form of our energy dedicated to this thing will live on and grow and matter)—and at the same time that it will end in the short run (that we will not be exerting ourselves ceaselessly). Take a conversation with a friend. Think how good it feels to speak your heart—then listen to theirs—back and forth for an hour or more. But then at some point the intensity needs to be balanced out with lightness. Yang needs yin. Words need space in the margins. Noise needs silence. The conversation ends, and both people look forward to continuing it at a later time. With most things, we need to know when they are finished. For a session of writing or other deep work—when does it end? I can write well and hard until breakfast—then I rest. For a day of being an active and engaged parent—when do you have a quiet hour of solo? When is bedtime? These markers of reset are vitally important. I like to have a few throughout the day.

Layering activities can form a lovely triangle of reset buttons: each new activity marks an end to the previous activity and brings out a new form of energy. I find that layering brings its own form of rest, and in this way, as long as I balance my days, I rarely burn out. I cannot write indefinitely, because soon it will be time to parent; I cannot parent indefinitely, because soon it will be time to teach; I cannot teach indefinitely, because soon it will be night, and I must go to bed early enough to wake and write. In this way, living three lives in one can be more energizing than working to the wall with only a single life. I lean fully into each one until it is time to reset.

Do you see different layers in your own life that can offer relief from each other and balance each other out? Notice where one replenishes the soil left depleted by the other. Notice where one makes you look forward to the next. Notice how they build together. It comes down to this: We are all capable of living many lives during our time on earth, but we cannot live all of them at once.

Having a reset time ensures that everything is harvested and resown at a predictable time each year, month, week, day. It keeps life from losing form into habit over the years.

EVOLVE OR PERISH

"Evolve or perish," my ninety-year-old friend says of this imperative to edit with the seasons and make one's true self portable between them. She, over the years, has been forced to edit much. She has lived in many houses, called many cities home, suffered many losses, but she still can smile at the other end of it.

"Evolve or perish," all animals know. A hermit crab must change shells or die. I have kept hermit crabs as pets. They startle and flinch back into their shells when touched, but then they gain confidence and will walk on your hand. If you get them wet, they lift their small, hard bodies out of their shell as far as they can go while still holding on with their tail. If you scatter slightly bigger shells in their tank, in the secret hours of night they will move into them. There are so many ways to live. So many ways to align our shell with our soft innards. You can keep land and spread out on its acreage. You can fold into an apartment in an urban area and keep your shoes in the oven. You can live in a house far away from town and go to town as an outing. You can wake up and walk into town and say hello to all the people as you go.

We are dissolved into ashes by the end. What of the life we lived? An ordinary life, a good life, gets smaller and smaller, like a boat on the horizon, remembered by each generation with fewer facts, until finally it is gone. Certain extraordinary lives get remembered as folklore, but it is usually for the ways we impacted others or what great love or work we left behind. Not for the stuff. So what is it for, then? Before I learned to edit well, I remember leaving college with a huge, heavy closet, more than I could pack into several suitcases. "Who owns whom?" my Italian friend asked. "I think your things own you more than the other way. Why are you carrying all of this around?"

When I feel stuck it means I've outgrown my current shell. I feel an ugly twist in my upper body when my external life and my internal self don't match. When I listen, this feeling guides me. Sometimes it takes me a long time to listen. Generations of discipline and hard labor bred into me, I try to work through discomfort first, without pausing to ask: Am I the problem? Or is it my current shell? Sometimes I'm the problem. Sometimes it's the shell. It's a game of constant attention.

SEASONS ALLOW US TO EXPAND AND CONTRACT

There are seasons of retreat and simplicity, seasons of abundance. We are familiar with many of the wise souvenirs produced of these seasons of retreat: Henry David Thoreau built a tiny cabin for himself by Walden Pond where he lived alone two years. Diogenes moved into a barrel in the agora (marketplace), where he could be in the world of ancient Athens but not *of it*. Karl Jung kept a busy clinical psychology practice in lively Vienna but retreated each weekend to his gaslit country house in the woods. Anne Morrow Lindbergh stayed summers for two weeks alone in a small beach house, where she rolled up the rugs so as not to be distracted with housework and spent nights lying on the sand and looking up at the great "bowl of stars"; in this way she wrote *Gift from the Sea*.

Each of these retreats came to an end, as all do—even in the lives of habitual vagabonds, there are moments of touching down, moments of connecting to something that means "home," even if it doesn't look like your home or mine. But each one is a season of distillation. Often it requires some form of retreat from complicated, ordinary, messy life—as the Shed has been, in part, for us—so that we can reenter life with more energy, more wisdom, more *life* to offer.

In moving to the Shed, we decided for an indefinite season to distill into what we hoped would feel like purer forms of work, love, and play. Retreat out of management mode, worry, housework (especially the machines: dishwasher, clothes washer), hunting for lost objects, constant applying for and taking on odd jobs for money alone—those things feel neither pleasurable nor productive. So we shed them. We would dwell well, instead. We would try it for a season.

In moving to the Shed, we wished to try to reconcile some seemingly impossible opposites: How to live with simplicity—not just for retreats, short bands of time away, but as a general rule—while still living within the community and being of use? How to be a relentless seeker—while maintaining a home? How to live a big, fascinating, story-worthy life—while still showing up daily for work? How to be wildly unshackled from the constraints of the clock—and still get my children to school on time?

It can all be possible, I believe, when we balance seasons of leaning into the world with seasons of distilling. Expand, contract. Season of participation, season of sabbatical.

Even Thoreau, who shunned civilization for two years while living at Walden Pond, came back to live as a "sojourner in civilized life" to write and lecture about what he learned. He did not remain at the pond forever. The world is made—and unmade—and, we hope, eventually improved—by those who participate in it. By those who respect their own seasons.

Many people are now saying that despite the fear and economic loss, the season of the pandemic has brought them closer to their core values. They have spent more time (even over Zoom) with the people they love most, doing the work they must do, and letting everything else fall. They have exercised more, pursued hobbies; writers have written, makers have made; they have dug down deep into their home and garden. People have felt lucky to have what they have; people have survived without things they once depended on.

This is what happens when the season changes. We feel first resistance, but then gratitude and ease, more ease than we can remember feeling before. It is a renewal of the vow we have made to our life. A new shell! Like any shell, it will have a season. It hurts the heart to think of moving on from a shell that we love. It should. But it is one of the ironies of life that when we are most comfortable is often when shedding time is near.

By respecting each season and recognizing that it will come to an end, we stay fully awake to our lives.

LIFE-EDIT PROMPTS

1. **Create seasonal routines: one in, one out.** What are your current seasonal routines, both great and small? Are there seasonal routines you like the idea of? Try to implement a new routine each season, and cull out an old one that no longer serves you. One in, one out.

2. **Set yourself a brave thing.** Set a big one: In which direction does it feel necessary for you to grow in order to feel like you are living your best life? What is one big thing out of your comfort zone—the brave thing—

you can try to do once, perhaps with the company of a trusted guide or friend? Make it a goal. And set a small, brave thing: If you wish to be more outgoing, perhaps it is to say hi to one stranger a day. If you wish to feel more connected to your family, can you put on your calendar to call a few family members each month, just to say hi? If you are afraid of swimming, how about signing up for lessons?

3. **Write your credo.** One of the most valuable actions I've ever taken is to write a credo. I keep it framed on my desk, even a decade after writing it. It details who I am as a writer, what I prioritize, and who I wish to be. Write yourself a personal credo for this season of your life—maybe a year, maybe a decade. Let it be a sort of template for living that you can return to (and edit) over the years. Let it describe the essence of who you are and who you wish to be in this season.

4. **Set a season-change day.** Put on your calendar a "season change" day three or four times a year: a day or a week where you change out clothes, swap out objects (such as in the fall, swap the snow-cone maker for the Crock-Pot, or put on snow tires, or change out summer sheets for flannel ones), clean off your desk, evaluate routines. Even if you live in a place without natural seasons, such a day is useful not only for putting

away seasonal objects but also for adjusting interior ways of being, such as times for waking and sleeping, expectations for self and others, and daily habits and comforts.

5. **Find the value in season, reason, or life.** Banish guilt about an object or routine that was of vital importance to you in an earlier season, but that in your heart you have moved on from. You can thank it silently in your mind or think of it with fondness. Consider too your friendship in these three categories. It is always tempting to promise "We'll catch up when we come up for air!" But is this really what you want? Know that you are free to say "Goodbye—thank you for this afternoon together!" without making next-time promises or getting out calendars. Does that thought feel strange or freeing? Both? Try it and see what feels true. This exercise reminds us that any promise we make is a choice, and that we do not have to say forever to anything or anyone unless we mean it.

6. **Set a streak.** Is there some streak you would enjoy implementing for a season? I like for my streaks to combine two things I enjoy and want to do more of: for example, having interesting conversations with strangers + writing poems = Poetry for Strangers. Yours could be a dinner party streak. Or a streak of going to

the zoo each Sunday morning with your early-waking child. Or playing cards Friday nights with your parents. Or running or writing or tap-dancing. Let the streak end when it ends—the beauty of a streak is that you do not feel the need to do it forever. But you will get to keep the memory of having enjoyed it intensely for an era.

7. **Identify the emotional souvenir.** Look for the beauty in a difficult era in your life. What was the emotional souvenir? What do you remember fondly? Try to do this again and again so you have something (however small) to remember with gratitude from each era. Now look at this era: What is worth preserving/guarding in your own life today? How can you highlight it and shape your days around it so that you can give it breathing room?

8. **Find reset buttons.** Are there natural points in the cycles of your work, love, and play when you can take a moment and reset? Try to find one each day, each week, each month, each season, each year. Make a list of reflective questions you might ask yourselves at these intervals, the simplest being "What do I love? What fills my time?" Write these reset dates on your calendar or somewhere you will find them.

6

EDIT FOR GENEROSITY

Adding to the Green

When we eliminate spending—of energy, time, money—that does not align with our essential loves and needs, we see more clearly what we wish to produce, what beautiful or useful thing we can add to the green of the world. Or put another way: We are better able to ask little and give much. To show up with more—more cheer, more attention, more utility, more patience, more wine—than we intend to take.

The green is what we leave growing. The green can be one's children, grandchildren, one's creative work, one's community, or one's encouragement. We add to the green by our work, our play, our love. If we create something that moves or helps people, we add to the green. If we feed people, connect with people, nurture ideas that sprout actions—we add to the green. By shifting energy from "mine" to "ours," we invariably add to the green. If we think of our money, our work, our power, and our ideas as tools for adding to the green, we invest in the world that will outlast us.

Children are a good example of this, for they add to the green in nearly everything they attempt, if left to their own devices. They make things—art, games, projects, and performances—and they offer them as gifts to others. Often, we who are no longer children are too busy to stop and take notice. But when we add to the green, acknowledgment may be the only thing we seek in return: someone to notice and say, "I see that you added this. I appreciate it. Thank you." Humans do not add to the green because we want something in return; rather, we add our small contribution to the world because it feels good to do: it is rewarding and it gives us a feeling of purpose.

I believe we add to the green through engaging our whole self, our work, love, and play.

A year before he died, my dear poet friend Gary Cooke said, when I asked him what he thought was the best use of a life, "Oh, I don't know, Elisabeth. I think all we can do is take in as much beauty as we can and try to add a bit back."

I have thought of his words many times over the years. I believe that this philosophy can distill to a meaning of life triangle between what gives you joy and pleasure on a day-to-day basis (your play), how you wish to leave a positive impact on the world (your work), and who you are connected to (your love).

I used to get into funks, sort of short-term depressions, as a younger woman. I'd wonder: What is my use? What am I doing with my life? Instinctively the solution was to rekindle access to my work, love, and play—and find a way for them to add to someone else's green. Now anytime I feel tired or out of sorts, I do this preventatively. Call someone or send a message to say hello. Do some small amount of meaningful work. Do something with my hands and share it. Have a treat! And exercise, obviously. A funk is simply a rut where you don't feel you are adding to the green of the world. Knowing these essential lodestones can help us work our way back. They can tip our self-focus into more generous other-focus, which releases us. The following life-editing practices can help too.

A GREAT LIFE QUESTION

Each of us has the ability to be propelled out of bed by some question that the day holds in suspense. In a way this question is the soul's question: your *ikigai*. I found that word in my readings about centenarians who find joy and meaning in their lives well past age one hundred. It is an Okinawan term that means "reason for being": the intersection of what you love, what you are good at, and what the world needs.

I love to write poems, but the world needs inspiration and simplification. How can I use what I know and love of poem-writing to inspire others to help simplify? You might be able to weave an argument out of any facts—how can you use this to defend those who need it? You might be able to build anything out of wood.

What can you build—and for whom? You might have an ability to see possibilities in anything: a room, an outfit, a day. What can that vision illuminate on a grand scale?

This, then, is the question that your life is trying to answer. You know the question, even if it is hard to articulate. A great life question will work at two levels, individual and societal: it will feel good to us, and it will serve the world beyond us. If our question only works at one level—benefiting the individual—it fails. The reverse is true as well.

Linking our individual lives to the broader world is a constant practice in attention and hope. I try to ask myself and my children daily: "What do you wish to add to the green?" I try to live the answer to this question—and I fail, and try again. But I keep asking, because this question inspires me to live well.

My questions are things such as: Will I prepare my kids for adulthood so they will practice being their best selves—and add to the green? Will I write something that benefits my world? Will I teach in a way that inspires other writers to create brilliant, lasting work and to support each other? Will I care for my body well so I can maximize its health in the ways I can control? Will I honor my friends' needs so that our friendship can bridge the years—can we add to each other's green? Will I find ways to be creative, to play, to be curious? Will I enjoy this hour, this day, so that I don't look back on my life and feel regret that I missed living it? We pose these questions, and we do our best to answer them with the ways we live our lives.

One friend's version of this question that she tries to ask herself at night is: *Have I connected today (to myself, my work, my people)?* Where can we spread the good stuff—joy, knowledge, acceptance— in outward-moving ripples? How can we serve as models, even only for a few people? It is worth asking ourselves what green we can add, given our skill sets, interests, limitations, and the state of our world today. How can I be of use? What can I help to grow? By set-

---

What can I help to grow?

---

ting a great life question, we can look to it for guidance, especially on the days when we need it most. A great question, if we answer it with our life, will invariably create a great life.

ACCEPT YOUR SUPERPOWER(S)

One time in my thirties, I was invited to join a super-scholarly academic book club. After puzzling over it for a week, I asked the person who invited me: Why exactly have I been invited, since we all know that I'm not a proper scholar? His answer I will remember forever: "Yes, I know that. But you are good for the soul." With that information in mind, I showed up without any worry that I was not intellectually adding to the group—the group was full of intellectual powerhouses! My job was *not* to say the smartest thing about our book. My job was to show up in good spirits and keep things easygoing and fun. In short, this was my superpower, the green I added to this particular group.

My husband has a number of superpowers, one of which is leadership. Organizing groups of people and planning events, however ordinary or extraordinary—he can do it. My dad's superpower is a sort of Labrador-ish contagious cheerfulness. One of my mom's superpowers is to see what needs to be done and learn the skills to do it; also to look for the cliff's edge in any situation and help people see how they might proactively avoid certain undesirable outcomes. One of my mentors has a magical quality of introducing people to each other: just the right people, at just the right times. I like to watch my children's superpowers over the years, sometimes changing, sometimes continuous. My daughter has been a maker all her life, and one of her current superpowers is to use her art to help our family celebrate holidays. I find paper wreaths for Easter, handmade pop-up valentines and birthday cards, all written in her careful cursive. My son's superpower has always been to make anyone laugh—even going through airports, he says things in passing that leave TSA employees looking at each other in amazed giggles. He can cheer anyone up. He is a bully melter: around him, playground bullies regularly reverse tactics and play nicely, because he can create, without any apparent effort, an environment in which everyone feels included and is having fun.

Each of my students has a superpower—and part of my work as their teacher is to identify it and draw it out. One is a community builder: she mobilizes the class to be a unit, full of friends and supporters who meet outside of class hours. One is a connector: he thinks about how his classmates' writing can find homes in the world, and he introduces people who might be able to help each other. Another is a genius reader who can always see what each piece of work is essentially about before the rest of us can.

What is your superpower? I suspect you have more than one. What feels effortless to you? Where does your energy naturally flow? What do you bring to a group? It may be something you do in your free time, for fun, that is innate to you. Organize? Connect? Create? Nourish? Theorize?

What is your superpower?

It is worthwhile to try to define the green for each of your different life areas; doing so offers straightforward ways we can form the questions that guide our daily decisions. It also helps us claim our mastery.

Now that I am a teacher, I tell my students that their writing should put forth an idea that promotes critical thinking and that in turn leads to the betterment of society. This is a tall order. But why create anything, in writing or in life, that does not try to heal the world in some small or large way? We see an inspiring thing, and we want to add something inspiring of our own. Receiving any kindness creates energy to put forward a new kindness.

One of the great freedoms of our lives is our ability to consider what service we can offer, what small piece we can add to the whole picture, what way our interests can intersect with what the world could use, appreciate, or need. One of my friends is a politician who gets through the elections that don't go her way by reminding herself and her friends to "double down on your thing. Don't try to do everything. If your thing is to write letters and knock on doors to get voters involved, then do it. But if your thing is to do something else, then do that."

Rather than going crazy trying to show up for every single rally, when rallying is not really my thing, I am reminded by her words to pick what I can add and accept my mastery of it, without wishing that it be something else. I am a writer: Perhaps I can raise my writing to add to the green of the world. Teachers can teach. Builders can build. Parents can parent. Scientists can conduct experiments and promote scientific knowledge. And so on. Do your own work well and in line with what you believe, to the extent that you can. Life is always a balancing act.

Life is always a balancing act.

Here is what my superpower is not: home improvement.

I don't know how to fix things, whether with chain saws and screwdrivers and molly bolts (James's realm) or a needle and thread (Cora's) or even tape and a hot-glue gun (Scott's). When I move into a dwelling and survey the existing walls and carpets, I think, *Well, this is it.* But I know how to fix things with words. This, I think, is my best superpower: creativity and communication. A long car ride leads to a made-up game. If there is a lull in conversation, with ease I can offer a new subject. I can talk my way through a lot of situations. When traveling with the children, even when they were babies, if we ended up on the wrong bus, it would become an adventure and quite likely we'd make a friend along the way. When camping with friends (being useful in the wilderness is far from my superpower, but it is one of James's many) and the kids get bored and mischievous, I can whip up a scavenger hunt in minutes, complete with rhyming clues. I can tell a story. With this form of creativity comes the superpower of improvisation: If we have no money, I think up free fun. When we have a seemingly empty kitchen, I can still make soup out of what looks like thin air. If we have no birthday gift and a party starting in twenty minutes, I can make a charming gift card to invite the birthday child over to our house to make chocolate-covered strawberries—and we have a lot of fun doing so. If there are no fresh flowers and there should clearly be fresh flowers, I can hike for fifteen minutes and come back with a beautiful foothills bouquet. "I am driven by laziness and quality," one of my friends observed of himself. I suppose I am too.

I have found ways for my superpower to come in handy, especially out in the world and in a tiny house. Not every contingency can be planned for, but most can be handled well through improvisation. Combine this skill with the handy skills of the rest of my family, and voilà! It works.

My guess is that your superpowers, like mine, are different from those of your friends and family. Capitalize upon those differences. What is your individual, unique mastery, however small or strange it seems? Claim it like the superpower it is.

CHANGE OBLIGATIONS INTO GIFTS

When we moved to the Shed, I set boundaries around how many hours I would work each day, and what to expect of myself each year in terms of work obligations. I began a practice of connecting prospective clients, whose work I would not take on, to other writers and editors I admired, including my students—creating opportunities for them while also remaining a resource in my community. My own mentors had done this for me many times over many years—given meaningful work that they did not need or want to their protégés like me, who needed and welcomed those opportunities. Now it was my turn to do the same.

The moment I cleared my desk, so to speak, indicating I was ready, exciting new work came. Opportunities in the form of grants, collaborations with artists I admire, random calls out of the blue asking me to teach a class on this or that aspect of writing. New ideas came too: many writers speak of "taking dictation" when they write—the brain, spinning out the project while we rest, simply flings us good lines and we jot them down. This began to happen to me, I think primarily because I hadn't jam-packed all the avenues for good ideas to emerge. Once I realized that I did not need as much money as I thought I did, or at least not enough to make it worthwhile to take on work that was not my first choice, creativity came back. I doubled down on the one teaching job I loved, and asked for more classes there.

And I realized a solution to the marketing problem that many writers face, one that I had been facing too. Writers today are expected to spend hours each week advertising their books, something I had taken classes on how to do, but really, *really* didn't enjoy doing: for not only was I adding clutter of words to the world (words that are not necessary or beautiful) but also I was entering an arms race. My general practice is to try to opt out of arms races, whether of knowledge, showing off, or the spy vs. spy game of advertising.

Lightening my load of work created space for an alternative idea. Rather than hocking my wares, I would give gifts. I would invite writing clients, past and present, to a winter solstice writing session; we'd sit by the fire and drink mulled wine and I'd guide us in a series of freewriting exercises. The spirit of the gift felt alive too in my weekly Poetry for Strangers project; for a writer, writing a weekly poem to share with the community guarantees several things: a steady stream of new words (I've had to look some up), the vulnerability and fun for me of having to constantly make new acquaintances, the imperative to write poems that matter to ordinary people, and an enthusiastic group of poetry fans waiting each week to see what poem would come.

To this I added a weekly gift involving my children: I would go each week into my children's classes and tell the tiny students fairy tales, my favorite type of stories. Einstein is supposed to have said: "If you want your children to be intelligent, read them fairy tales; if you want them to be more intelligent, read them more fairy tales."

These stories are about problem-solving as a way to come of age; it seemed a fun way to get these tiny children thinking critically and creatively about the ways they would be called upon, in life, to add to the world. Being the Fairy Tale Mom meant that I could know their classmates and teachers, and volunteer in a way that felt meaningful to me (rather than organizing the Lego bin or keeping watch at recess, neither of which play to my strengths). Having "gift" replace "obligation" feels right; it is a way to life-edit through sharing what you love or what you already do well.

There are so many ways to do this. Consider how you can turn your obligations into something that adds to the green. Say you have an obligation to walk your dog three times a day—perhaps you could turn a walk into a gift by offering to bring a neighbor's dog while she works long days. Say a friend is struggling to get dinner on his table and you always lament at throwing away leftovers—can you bring over a meal or two each week? Neither one is any more work than what you are already doing, and either one spreads kindness.

This life-edit can descend into the less conscious realms too. What emotional obligations do you ask yourself to bear? Two of mine are feeling the need to carry every conversation (which sometimes leads to nobody else getting a word in) and also the need to analyze a situation once it's happened—label it good or bad or funny or sad or some emotional "tag." I wonder what conversations and revelations might come if I were to practice replacing those obligations with a gift instead, such as a smile, or a generous pause to let the other person speak.

Or can you give the highest gift—the gift of trust and autonomy—to your partner or children or housemates, so that they can do things for themselves that you ordinarily do, which lightens your load of obligations at home, in addition to empowering them?

Don't torture yourself with any of this, obviously. A gift should feel good to give.

EMBRACE THE MINIMUM (COMFORTABLE) ENVIRONMENT

It seems so many have come to this same conclusion, that to add the most to the world we must content ourselves with having the least: Leonard Cohen said in an interview, "The minimum environment that would enable you to do your work with the least distraction and the most aesthetic deliverance came from a modest surrounding. A palace, a yacht would be an enormous distraction from the project . . . I liked living in a little shack." Case in point: Google, Microsoft, Apple, HP, and Amazon all got their starts in garages! Much of my own best writing has happened in an office the size of a phone booth, too small for anyone else to enter. Humans have done a lot with a little over the years.

But certain forms of richness come at the cost of others. Tom Hodgkinson of *The Idler* has quite rightly observed that if you content yourself with the technology of ten years ago, you will live like a wealthy person, and if you content yourself with the technology of a hundred years ago, you will live like a king. Remember, though, that royalty had staffs. But most of us are the staffs for our own houses. We have to work, we have to tend our own relationships, we have to exercise our own bodies. Which brings us around to Picasso's way of looking at it: "I'd like to live as a poor man with lots of money." He added to the green immensely, changing art forever.

Indeed, from an add-to-the-green perspective, there is little value to owning costly things. These things we must manage and contend with, and often they distract us from our life's work. Time and again, we see the need to create in simplicity, in humble conditions. Stephen King tells a story about abandoning his showy desk for a humbler corner desk, where his corgis like to curl. To create anything involves play, or some form of it: we play when we are exploring, when we are curious and pushing against boundaries—and not when we are fearfully guarding the status quo, afraid to lose something or to fail. Antithetical to play is the feeling of defense we get when we are protecting something, conserving something, trying to feel worthy of something that we could lose (such as the big desk in the center of our study, at which we are not writing).

It is something of an "Emperor's New Clothes" problem. Had the emperor contented himself with ordinary threads, he would not have let his empire go cold and hungry; his story would not have ended in the humiliation of standing naked at his own parade. He is a fiction, but a useful fiction; we all know people who turn power into a tool for "me" and not "us." Many of these people go so far as to discredit anything that looks hopeful or possible. This is a form of burning the green. But from ashes things grow. They say even God did the best creating in an empty dark void.

HEAL THE WORLD

I mentioned my thoughts about adding to the green to a Jewish friend, who said with recognition in his eyes, "*Tikkun olam!*" He then explained, "It means to heal the world. It is what we all try to do, both individually and as a group." A literal form of healing the world is letting green be green. Letting the green replace the gray we have paved over the green with. This metaphor both sustains and haunts me.

Many people feel that they must choose which green they add—we cannot add all the green we wish to add at once! A nurse friend wonders: "Which of the two causes I care about most do I work for in my limited time?" She feels torn between two: racial equality and women's reproductive freedom. She also has three children and a full-time job. For her, choosing only one cause feels like an impossible choice. But whether she works on one for ten hours a week this year, then switches the next year; or each one five hours; or one forever—she is adding to the green. When we add to the green, other green grows from it. Sometimes we will have to choose one form now, one later. This too is a part of editing.

It is tempting to ask: Can one life make a difference? Yes, but that question is not what should keep us awake nights. What we get immediately from adding to the green is the self-respect that comes with knowing our actions and joys are not ones that make trouble for the universe. That today, and yesterday, and the day before, we added one small, kind thing. That we have lived honestly by our own standards and as well as we can live, given the parameters of who we are.

I arrived at my choice of lives—writer, teacher, mother—because I enjoyed them and because I felt I could do them well. In enjoying them, I have become better at each. I feel that I have something to add, and my act of adding has something to teach. But such adding requires deep focus. Having smaller boundaries in some aspects (home) has freed up energy to have infinite variety and freedom to create in others (work, love, play). Minimizing my needs (my internal focus) would, then, allow me to add more freely to the green—to shift my focus externally.

Whenever I get overwhelmed with the question of where my energy should go, I have to remember that it's not just teaching, writing, or raising children that I'm doing: in short, it's rebuilding the world through love.

ADD IN TREATS (AND LOOK BELOW FOR THE "REAL TREAT")

My daughter, three years older than my son, has had a lot of capital-L "Lessons" (which we also call "nameable activities," unlike cardboard creations or stuffed-animal performances). This means that once a week for much of his life my son has a blank hour waiting with me at the swimming pool or dance studio or outside the music teacher's room. I used to think of these as waiting hours. Lessons interrupted his naps, exhaling us from the house at inconvenient times. But looking closely at those hours, I was able to see some opportunities for unexpected green in the form of time with my sweet son. He goes with whatever flow. He doesn't mind. But when given the chance to flow in his own direction, he will amaze me. The gift of Lessons was that it was just him and me.

I started to think of those hours or half hours as our dates. When he was a baby, a date might be simply a walk around the block to look for backhoe diggers, or a trip up the escalator. As he got older, they evolved, first into café dates (my favorite!) for croissants and hot cocoa. But eventually as her Lessons got longer, he and I started to do some pretty interesting stuff—his own seeking, not his sister's. For example, during Cora's three-hour sailing lesson, Scott and I got into a lovely routine of sitting in the sailing club, writing a book together. He dictates, I transcribe. His usual genre is horror/romance, which is not a genre I'd otherwise think to write. After writing, we go for a walk along the docks.

"Have you had enough of everything?" I asked him one evening after we had written a new chapter of his book, *The Wolves of the Wild*; we had had fries and lemonade and for me a lovely beer; we had walked up and down the dock, looked at fish, explored a cave.

"Of course not!" he said, as if I had asked a ridiculous question. Then he clarified: "I just love this so much!"

So do I.

My dates with my son during Lessons built up our relationship significantly because we both pursued contentment together. Treats of time with people are one thing. Solo treats are another. Your work is to add to the green of the world; your treats help build up the contentment inside of you. What always cheers you up? These are your treats.

We all know that the majority of life's great pleasures come cheap: conversation, thinking, nature—for me add writing and walking, and I've got just about all I could ask for. Often, I need a small treat to bring me to the larger treat: a promise of a massage after meeting a deadline; a coffee and a muffin as a lure to the writing desk at 6:00 a.m. A family movie after cleaning the house. Meeting a good friend at the museum so we can look at all the important stuff together and talk while we do. Bribery works wonders, primarily if to hitch the good habit (writing, running, cleaning house, learning) to the desired treat. Whatever you lure yourself with, you will follow that carrot until you finish the race. Best to stack treats early in the day, I find. When we do it right, the entire day feels like a series of treats. Wake up looking forward to the world.

Wake up looking forward to the world.

The truth that we of course know is that the treats are not the real treat. Time with my son is the real treat; French fries are the topical treat that gets us sitting down together at the sailing club table. Coffee and a muffin are the topical treat; it is a lifetime of waking up doing my chosen creative activity that is the real treat. But for many people, treats can go a long way in making the pleasure of the activity concrete and for bringing our bodies to the table.

Consider which treats add to the green of *you*. What makes your superpowers glow, and makes you feel like you can do anything with ease? What topical pleasure gives you back your energy enough to do deeper things that become major and ongoing energy sources? For me it's a warm drink, warm socks (topical)—which give me energy to engage in a good conversation or writing session (major energy sources). For my daughter, it's learning a new craft from an online tutorial—which gives her energy to make beautiful paper gifts for the people she loves (major energy source).

When my son was a newborn, my husband, daughter, and I made lists of small things we enjoy: our pleasures. The ways we like to use our free time. My daughter's included snuggling with the dog, making art, eating cereal with me(!). My husband's list included more time-intensive outdoor adventures such as skiing, swimming, fishing. We posted them all on the fridge, knowing that having a new baby would disrupt our lives quite considerably, and that having these lists in plain sight would provide us with a quick list of treats for when the baby was napping (Cora and I could snuggle with a book and both feel replenished afterward, rather than my whiling away the napping hour on housework, giving her my phone to play with). It helped us feel connected to our pleasures and able to take care of the baby as a family; it was a sort of insurance against feeling depleted or aimless in those consuming early months.

Now I do this out of habit, without thinking. I keep a mental list of "good uses of time" or five-minute "Elisabeth treats." If a student is late for a Zoom meeting and I find myself feeling my time and energy drain away while I wait, I send an email to the student saying when I'll be back and go do five minutes of stretching, or I send a kind email to someone, or make a cup of tea and eat a glorious Medjool date. In short, I use treats as microdoses of green to reset the plan away from annoyance and toward patience and kind energy, so that I can show up with my best version of myself, ready to offer something of value.

LIFE-EDIT PROMPTS

1. **Map out your *ikigai*:** What is your *ikigai*, your reason for going into the day? The answer will live at the intersection of what you love, what you are good at, what the world needs, and, perhaps, what the world will pay you to do. You might try to draw Venn diagrams (four intersecting circles) to list out answers in each of these circles, seeing where they intersect. How can the essence—or the specifics—of something you love and are good at be of value to the world? List some ways.

2. **Ask your great life question.** Try to write, in as many forms as you need, your great life question about what green you can add to the world. Remember, your great life question will work at two levels, individual and societal: It will feel good to you, and it will serve the world beyond you. It will link your small individual life to the great big world. What can you do tomorrow to try to live out the answer to that question? What can you do this year?

3. **What is your superpower?** Give yourself a badge for it (even an invisible one). What is something you can always do well? Are you invariably helpful and graceful in a crisis? Are you good at thinking ahead so that you avoid crises? Either of these is useful. What is your superpower in each of your life's circles? Claim your mastery of that power. Abdicate the need to be recognized for other powers that don't come naturally.

4. **Make your pleasure list.** And tack it to the fridge! What do you always enjoy doing? Refer to this list when you have small spots of time during the day. List both short and long pleasures, topical and deep ones. Your work is to add to the green of the world; your treats and pleasures help add to the green of *you*. What always cheers you up? List some things, even if they are small or feel silly. Think of ways to build them in. They will replenish you and help every day feel like a treat.

Can you give yourself several small treats a day, and a big treat each month? Can you refer to this list when you have small bits of free time (rather than doing something that does not replenish you)?

5. **The minimum (comfortable) environment.** What is yours? I feel I can do pretty much anything in the world if I have hot water and a clean bed. Look around your house. What do you need the best of, and what can you do without? Maybe you don't need a dining room, but love to be surrounded by art on the walls. Maybe you can happily share a bathroom, but you like to have an office all your own. Is there a way to distill your environment and home needs to precisely what you need in order to do your life's work?

6. **Your world's healing needs.** Is there something immediately outside yourself that you can do something about? Think broadly and deeply—what or who needs healing and attention inside your house, inside your neighborhood, inside your community or profession, inside your world? Consider doing one small kind thing to help repair it: to add your skill, your wisdom, or your kindness to the green.

PART 3

Enjoy Your Life

7

ENJOY THE ORDINARY DAYS

Organizing in Orbits

By now, you have done the hard part. You have looked at your life closely; you have chosen which edits feel necessary to make, based on what matters to you. In short, you've rewired your life, in big or small ways, to fit what matters to you. You've done this to the best of your ability now. You have these tools in your toolbox for other seasons, when you can edit further if you wish. But for now, you've edited. Now what's left is to enjoy your life.

For many, this can be the hardest part. The being in the here and now; the trusting the systems; the gratitude and the light steering. As my pilot friend says, the hard part is getting the airplane up and down. Now you can coast. But there is an art to coasting. Chekhov put it this way: "Any idiot can face a crisis. It is the day-to-day living that wears you out." Now we will look at the day-to-day living.

There is an art to coasting.

PLAN TO BE SURPRISED; FOLD SURPRISES INTO THE PLAN

In the world of writing, there are considered to be two categories: plotters and pantsers. Plotters begin with a plan in mind and know where they are going. Consequently, they waste fewer words and take fewer false turns in the process than pantsers, called such for writing from the seat of their pants. Pantsers follow where the moment takes them, writing from a place of constant surprise and amazement. Pantsers may write an entire book to discover what their book is about, then rewrite from the beginning to get the plot right (or abandon the book and write another). Pantsers are free and spontaneous, while plotters are diligent and organized.

It is easy to see ourselves in this either-or. A well-edited life—and the full, deliberate days and years that come from it—derives from our constant ability to be both.

Research on how we remember suggests that anticipation is a pleasant and necessary part of remembering an experience in full. But so is being spontaneous, in the here and now, ready to respond to what life brings. We have a plan for the day, or the week, or the year, or the life—an aspirational container of sorts into which the known unknowns will fill.

A lawyer begins a cross-examination with a set of informed questions, then must be nimble enough to adapt according to the information learned. A teacher starts a semester with a syllabus and a class plan—and builds room into the classes for student questions and interests to shape the discussion. A vacation starts with a (somewhat) set itinerary (depends on who's planning!)—and then in the interstitial space between plans, accidents happen, encounters take place, and the surprising memories are made.

The plan for the project gets us off the ground, and when we go into flow while working on it, surprises will reveal themselves. In all of these examples, the plotter sets the parameters for the pantser to play within—and then the pantser's discoveries become fodder for the next (better) version of the plan, or of the result. The lawyer laces the findings all together into an argument for the jury. The teacher sums up the discussion in terms of what has been learned and plans the next day accordingly. The traveler looks back on the vacation and remembers both the planned and the unplanned. The project is a mix of what it was intended to be and what changed its course along the way. Many creative people I know have both planning days and spontaneous days. In the Shed, we often keep one weekend day scheduled and one day open.

In any version of this, there is a way to see both the possibilities for the day and the long-game plan. The trick is in plotting things out (to the best of one's ability and without going crazy) in the longer term, while simply living in the days. This model allows us to live spontaneously day by day, while feeling some semblance of living in the right direction.

BEGIN WITH THE END IN MIND: THE SOLAR SYSTEM MODEL

One way to find a balance between planning and surprise is to begin with the end in mind. We take care of today in any way we see fit, but at intervals we pause and think ahead and ask: *What do I want the end to look like?* In other words, if we do our best with today's "pantsing" in a direction that we have thought through, our overall life "plot" will be a good one.

For me, I know exactly: I got cajoled by a friend (who is much more plotter than I) into writing down my ten- and fifty-year(!) goals, and she was right: it felt useful and good to do—even if highly speculative. My goals are divided into the categories of work, love, and play, and my guess is that they look a lot like everybody else's: good relationships, healthy body, work that feels meaningful and fun and that pays well enough, adventure and comfort in just proportions. My specifics will be particular to my life, as will yours to yours, but at the end, each one can generally be distilled into long-term *future feelings* and short-term *daily actions*. But daily actions in each life area can build up and feel like *a lot* to do. Each day, each week, each month I must try to nurture one of those areas. How?

Meet the solar system model of organizing in orbits:

Say the innermost circle (or the sun) is today, here, now. Like the sun, our life today illuminates how we feel about our past and our future.

The next circle is the week, then the month, the season, the year, and so on. Look at your life spooling out in all directions—one direction is work, one is play, one is love, one is any number of values you hold dear. Think of each orbit as a container.

I think of this as the planetary method of organizing anything, whether clothes, food, relationships, work ambitions, or activities. By imagining life as a solar system, with today as the center, and the end of your life as the farthest reaches of outer space, we can hedge some bets about what we wish for "the end" to look like in each major life area.

Then we ask: What is the comfortable "unit" of things that can naturally fit into each circle of orbits: a day, week, month, year—provided we do our best to tidy as we go, and expect to be only imperfect? This method offers a visual map of ordinary life, so we can work toward our ideal life (in other words, we can plot) in a patient, reasonable way, often pantsing as we go.

This concentric-circle storage system is in great part how we manage to live in 275 square feet and generally not feel overwhelmed.

To use it, simply ask: What is necessary for me in this house this week?

This is the stuff of your daily life. It may be less than you think. For us, now, what belongs in the Shed includes the children's favorite stuffed animals (in their bed) and their current best drawings (on the art wall) and their Lego containers and art supplies (in small wooden boxes); our daily-use kitchen appliances; any exercise equipment, such as mats, bands, weights, that we are currently using (on the shelf above the adults' Murphy bed); and our current favorite books (on the bookshelf with the ladder affixed). These are the things that give us active joy or are necessary *now*, the things we would travel with on vacation, the things we require in order to conduct our daily life and would replace immediately if they were to break.

Every month or so, we survey what we have at home to see if there are any things—books, art, toys, too-small clothes—that belong for now in a different circle, and likewise any things from different circles that belong in the house.

Then the next orbit outward: What stuff do I need seasonally, or every few months? This belongs in our garage, in bins. This may be out-of-season clothes, formal wear, and athletic gear; pet supplies; the kids' swap-out toy bin; the kids' art portfolios (a container each for them to curate and preserve their favorite art creations); the seasonal or non-daily appliances; holiday items; and suitcases and camping gear, special-occasion things.

Then: What do I wish to keep but am okay not seeing for over a year? The answer to this question belongs in our final concentric circle. For us, this is a small storage unit thirty miles away, because we do not plan to live in the Shed forever; at some point the kids will grow up and not want to share a tiny camper-size Murphy bunk bed. This circle contains those things I wish to keep but can do without for five years or possibly forever. This is the stuff you either pass on to anyone who wants it or eventually toss.

The orbit system runs from most vital to daily life (in the house) to the least (storage unit). If you had to pack your life up in an hour, it'd be easy. Just because you have space, it is not necessary to fill it up with things that you don't love or use.

But of course, this system—like any good editing system—applies to much more than objects.

Love: Which people belong in my day? In my week? In my month? In my year? (Beyond a year gets a little fuzzy.) We cannot call every friend every day, but it is vital to systematically nourish the relationships that are most important to us.

Work: Which projects must I nudge forward each workday—and which ones require a big push every so often?

Health: Which foods and forms of movement belong in my days, and which in my weeks? Food might be a daily minimum of fruits and vegetables (and a maximum of less healthy foods), leaving room for an indulgent meal out or a dinner party every once in a while. Movement might be a short walk every day, making time twice a week for something else: a tennis game, a fitness class, weights at home. It could be a simple habit such as doing a ten-minute exercise sequence before breakfast, or a bit of stretching after a few hours of computer work, or even drinking a glass of water before getting to work.

Administration: Which tasks must happen daily? (Very few, it turns out.) Which ones monthly (such as paying bills); and which ones annually (financial planning, creating a work schedule, annual checkups)?

Using this model, we see that not everything has to happen now or belong in our house today. This allows our days to triage themselves into what is most vital. It may be that visualizing these circles is all you need to go forth deliberately into your ordinary days—or it may be that writing this out to make it concrete and actually filling in those items helps them become clear. Depending on the season, I find both useful.

When we have a too-large canvas for a life or when we lack an editing system, it is hard to determine what is important today, so all tasks—making food, doing work, making time for the people we love, answering emails—tend to fall into the same category: undone. By thinking of life as a series of concentric circles, we can prepare for both ordinary days and exceptions with ease and self-trust.

It is worth adding a few words here on some things that do *not* belong in your concentric circles—in other words, what one friend of mine calls her "not to do" list. For we did not edit our lives in order to later overfill them in ways that are different but still overwhelming or unaligned with our essential selves. You've culled a lot of energy drains. Don't invite them all back in. With your newfound freedom of time and energy, a shoddy way to spend it is on thinly disguised versions of the very things you've eliminated. A few of these vampires that I have to take special care not to open the door wide to are (1) frays and (2) over-research.

I categorize frays as any unproductive argument. Whether at town hall or online or with the neighbor, a fray happens when two or more people fail to mind their own business and end up bickering over each other's. A fray can disguise itself as a productive discussion toward finding a greater truth or a common ground, but it gives itself away when it becomes clear that neither side wishes to understand the other. I try to avoid frays at all costs, for they damage relationships and trust, and they move nothing forward.

Whenever I have free time and feel tempted to get involved in an argument "just for fun," I think of a funny old adage James used to say, a quote from an old song: "If you mind your own business, you'll stay busy all the time." In my experience, frays do not add to the green—mine or the world's—and so they do not belong in my day. When invited into a fray of any sort, I try never to take the bait. I have to believe that my time is more valuable than that. I have to believe that yours is too.

Over-research can be equally tempting and feel productive, but I find that it usually isn't. Over-research can catapult simple decisions into holy grail chases for a perfect answer, causing us to wander so far astray that we forget the question. I am embarrassed at how often I have fallen for this one! Sometimes I still do. Life is a work in progress. Whether trying to devise the perfect writing schedule or find the perfect water bottle, the principle ought to hold: Learn enough to make a good choice for now, but try not to overburden myself or my people or the decision itself with an overwhelming amount of information. My rule of thumb is that if I am worried about something, I should do enough research to learn more about it so that I can either change my habits or cease worrying—then I go do something else, something that does belong in my life's concentric circles. In short, we can dethrone the stress of a decision by taking it off its pedestal and giving it only a finite amount of our energy.

Knowing what belongs in your life today—and what does not—is the necessary first step to fully utilizing this tool. Then ask yourself, moving outward in concentric circles, what is necessary? (Other versions of this question: *What do I love? What gives me energy?*)

THE DAILY MINIMUM

There is a sequence in yoga called the daily minimum—it means the short practice that you do every single day, even if the day descends into chaos or even if, on certain days, you add to it further sequences. When I heard the term, I thought how useful it was. You might call it your "daily essentials." One of my classmates in graduate school used this principle and graduated long before the rest of us, simply by assigning herself five concrete tasks to do each day (one was to kiss her partner; one was to drink a huge bottle of water; another was to write forward in her dissertation; the other two varied with the day).

Big things in life are cumulative: the trust that love builds, the expertise work builds, the joy that compassion builds, the health that daily acts of wellness build—all of these accumulate throughout life. This is not to say that we cannot start fresh; sometimes we must. But doing a daily minimum—in other words, doing something small in each of these necessary areas—carries us a long way.

What is the daily minimum required for long-game success in any area of life: work, love, play, or health? My grandparents had one for love: They used to play a morning game of cribbage before he went off to the university. This was their daily twenty-minute fun—they played in the hospital the morning their first son was born. They played the last week of her life, after nearly seventy years of marriage. For a writer, the daily minimum might be writing for an hour, or until reaching an easily achievable number of words. For exercise, it might be doing twenty squats every day before brushing your teeth. For love, it might be kissing your mate, or reading to a child, or listening with full attention, without multitasking or interrupting, for five minutes. For a healthy diet, it might be to eat an apple before lunch, or a cup of berries with breakfast. The point of the daily minimum is that you do it, it counts, but it is extremely low stakes. And yet, it will anchor the day.

Here's my daily minimum, in order, starting as soon as I wake:

- Yoga or exercises (5–15 minutes)

- Write in my current book or in my journal (60–90 minutes)

- Triage student/client email (5–15 minutes)

- Eat breakfast with my family (30–60 minutes)

This is my morning routine, where my first flush of energy goes. Each of the four tasks falls into a specific category that is vital to my life: health, play, work, and love. When I miss too many days, I feel uprooted; so I begin again. At times I will take off a season—a week or a month or more—to sleep in and embrace the chaos; then soon I find myself returning to this daily minimum again, for it is a habit that feels good.

A day cannot contain all the elements that a life must contain—and there are days completely taken over by any number of unexpected and expected things. By editing to the basic elements that you want to be part of your whole life and by beginning your day with them, you can be open to what the day brings.

Most major religions have some translation of a phrase that roughly means "If you take care of today, you take care of your life." One of my favorites in this vein is by the Buddhist master Dainin Katagiri: "If you want to take care of tomorrow, take better care of today. We always live now." Rather than worrying about whether we will have strong bodies when we are older, we care for today by doing some exercise, by taking walks, by standing more and sitting less, by stretching while we talk on the phone or wait in line. Rather than worrying about whether we will have meaningful relationships with loved ones when we are older, we care for today by giving those people our best attention, even only for a few minutes, and by calling or writing those who live far away when we think of them.

"If you take care of today, you take care of your life."

How to remember these daily-minimum tasks as we are building the habit? My elementary school gym teacher had a good way: Each morning she put on her wrist eight rubber bands, which she would remove as she drank eight glasses of water. Now my son uses this trick, after he was constantly getting dehydrated. I have adapted this trick with a bracelet to remind myself to do a short bit of stretching or exercise each morning. I slide the bracelet on my right (dominant) wrist after brushing my teeth, and can move it to my left wrist once I've finished the job. The last thing I want is a bracelet—even a small rubber one—jangling around my dominant hand all day. So I get moving!

Small dorky tools, these tricks. But they work.

If we choose our first choices today, even in the smallest of ways, it is likely that we will have a life made of mostly first choices.

RESPECT YOUR TOMORROW SELF

Your today self is the bridge between your yesterday self and your tomorrow self. Accept the responsibility and privilege of being that bridge. Our yesterday self recognizes the need for these systems and sets the tasks. Our tomorrow self benefits from having done them. Our today self has the job of doing them.

The goal is to have a few good systems that help the rest feel like natural habits. Of course, there is and will be system overlap. Sometimes we must drop everything. But when we edit well, we do today's work today, in the most important order. As a consequence, we respect both our yesterday self and our tomorrow self.

This can be a hard one. Think how we assume that our tomorrow self will want to do all sorts of things that our today self has little interest in doing! This leads to procrastination and not trusting ourselves and our systems. It never feels good.

The best practice to respect the tomorrow self is to think from the end, backward to today: What do I want my life to have looked like? What should it contain? How do I feel? What matters? Plot it. Work back from there, as well as possible. I wish to have written a stack of books that have added to the green of the world; I wish to be good friends with my adult children and husband and friends and family; I wish to be proud of my students worldwide and still teaching in some form for my whole life; I wish to healthily and happily reach age one hundred, so I can enjoy as many good years as possible on earth. To maximize the probability of my success, there are certain things I know I must do this year, such as progress on a book, take care of my body, respect and listen to my people, and keep my teaching lively and enjoyable. These things can be broken down quite easily into tasks for today and tomorrow. Then the only work is to do them.

I also know that my life—like any life—has its own share of busywork. To keep it from taking over the stuff that matters, to respect my tomorrow self, I corral busywork into set times—like laundry day (Friday morning), or admin day (Friday morning too, while the laundry is going), or weekly financial meeting. That way the necessary busywork will not spill into the more valuable hours, or constantly feel undone and "on the list." It feels good to know where these recurring tasks live within my week—only then do they feel finite. I know when to tend them, when to ignore them. If leaving such things undone for even a day bugs you, try not to let it. As time expert Laura

Vanderkam has observed about housework, it is costly to hire some-one, but "it doesn't cost anything to lower your standards."

Everyone has some sort of personal system or credo, conscious or not. When we are conscious about creating systems with respect for our tomorrow self, we are more likely to follow them, for we understand why we are doing them. When it's laundry day, the right thing is to do the laundry, and by accepting this, even the laundry can feel like something of a finite pleasure. You won't want to do it tomorrow any more than you want to do it today, and presumably there will be something else that gets bumped tomorrow by procrastinating today's task. It can help to identify the block that has stopped the today self ("Laundry is boring") and the sacrifice that the tomorrow self will have to make if our today self snoozes on the job ("Tomorrow I'd rather be free to have a date with James").

Life is easier when we respect the containers or the boundaries, and when we fill them with care: that a day only holds twenty-four hours, a gestation requires nine months, a closet has room for only a certain number of hangers, or that you get tired and impatient at a certain hour of night, or that your knees hurt after walking four miles. Do not stuff life so full that you cannot remember yesterday or the day before, or that you spend today courting yesterday's regrets. Accept your parameters.

Accept your parameters.

CLEAN UP BY THE END OF THE DAY

This principle, taught to every kindergartener, is a game changer when applied to life. Cleaning up one meal is easy and offers a pleasing sort of closure; it finishes the occasion and creates a clean slate for the next meal. Cleaning up several days' worth of meals is miserably sticky and requires lots of scrubbing.

You can use this principle for people. If you and a family member argue, even if you have not yet come to an agreement, you can still make sure to do the bighearted thing of either apologizing if you think you were wrong, or saying, "I love you even though I am still angry"—or in some way seek to understand or call a truce for the night. We clean up by the end of the day when we do the kind thing before the day ends so the argument doesn't spill into the next day.

My grandfather, a former coal miner, said that cleaning up the mining site at the end of each day saves miners' lives.

Very luckily, most things that we leave undone today won't kill us tomorrow—but the principle carries much wisdom. In a less life-and-death way, I do this with my work. After teaching a class, I spend a few minutes making notes about what we covered and what we didn't—adding the latter to my class plan for the next time we meet, and adjusting my overall class plan to include any things we did in class or questions that arose that feel especially useful to bring up with future students. Ernest Hemingway ended a writing day mid-sentence so he could always pick up there: a form of closing up shop for the day by leaving a clear trail for tomorrow. Cal Newport in *Deep Work* describes having an end-of-work ritual. This too feels like a form of tidying up one activity before moving, with full attention, to another.

When our day splays out into the chaos that life inevitably breeds, it is worthwhile to choose one specific area to clean up before tomorrow. Our tomorrow self appreciates it.

MAKE THE UNCOMFORTABLE COMFORTABLE

A swimmer friend, who regularly goes into the freezing Atlantic without a wetsuit in January, has said of his swims: "It's a battle every time, but you get better at fighting it." In his early days he rewarded himself when he got out—with hot coffee, a bath, and a warm towelly cape that I tried on once and immediately coveted. But now he says the real reward is being in the water itself. Eventually, the thing you make into a habit will start to offer its own rewards.

Consider which acts or abstainings from acts will require the most discipline. Suffering is no fun for anyone—even though it can be generally instructive—but try to make your daily rituals (especially the difficult ones, the reaches) as comfortable as possible.

In luring myself to the writing desk, I simply won't go unless I feel warm: hot coffee, warm socks, and hot-water bottles all work for getting me to sit still for an hour.

What is uncomfortable for you?

If it's exercise—can you make it more fun by doing it with a friend, or promising yourself a lovely latte afterward, or a massage after you run twelve times? Or do you simply need a gym you like, or a fresh mat and band for working out at home? Give yourself these things.

If you loathe some administrative part of your job, can you add a comfort to it somehow? Bills and beer Tuesdays, anyone? Perhaps clean out your inbox in a room with a good view or at a table with a friend or with a fun date planned for afterward? Or claim a time of day for yourself that feels fresh and good when you can relax into these tasks? I found that the simple act of shifting my weekly admin to a café on Friday mornings, when I can listen to the pleasant buzz around me and have someone else make the coffee, gives me energy to do it early and quickly, and means that the rest of the weekend afterward feels uncluttered.

If you are trying to go to bed earlier, perhaps make your bedroom more appealing—take out anything with a too-bright light, or buy a pillow that feels good to use. Fresh sheets and a clean room go a long way.

If you wish to be more social but dread hosting, how can you make it easy for yourself? Potluck rather than you-do-all? Bring a meal to someone else's house, saving them the commute? Or invite people to meet at a park?

Can you make any of your commutes—to school, work, or regular engagements—more comfortable? I used to dread driving to work and battling the downtown parking—then I discovered the pleasure of simply catching the bus. Or—audiobooks! Think of how you might use the drive as thinking time, talking time, learning time, or any time you'd enjoy.

Do whatever it takes for you to make the uncomfortable comfortable.

With all of these together—or by just adapting your favorite one or two—you have a framework for enjoying ordinary days, being in the here and now without undue stress or worry, and keeping on with your well-edited life steered in the direction you have chosen.

LIFE-EDIT PROMPTS

1. **Align your inner plotter and pantser.** Make two lists: one of situations when you are by nature a plotter, and one for situations when you would prefer to go by the seat of your pants. Perhaps you love planning a vacation for months beforehand so that you get to live in it longer through anticipation. Or perhaps you are the opposite: you like to be in the present—live at home when you are at home—then show up on a vacation ready for anything. Consider whether these two lists are aligned with your life. You might take this a little further: Look back on a plan in your life that was waylaid in either a positive or a negative way—or both!—by a surprise. Track the major difference that the surprise made. How did the story end?

2. **Set your end goals (five years and ten years).** Write down your five-year and ten-year goals, divided into any categories you find useful (I like work, love, play, though you can be more specific). How will you feel, having met these goals? Who will you be if you act in their direction, using these goals as your life's compass? What daily, weekly, monthly, or yearly actions will help you become that person? For instance, if you wish to be a professional photographer, taking photos would likely go on the daily list; on the weekly list, perhaps planning (lightly) what you will photograph for the next week; on the monthly list, perhaps swapping your work with others to get feedback; and on the yearly list, perhaps setting aside a week to send out your best work to magazines or contests.

3. **Draw your life's solar system.** Draw a series of circles (see model on page 163—it looks a bit like an archery target). Place your goals—physical, family, professional, and the like—in their appropriate places: big goals on the outside of the outermost circle, day's work (or daily minimum) in the bull's-eye center. Do the balances feel right? Do weeks and seasons feel too heavy or too light? Adjust what fits in which circle until the balance feels right to you.

4. **Set your daily minimum.** Calculate how much time it will take in an ordinary day to meet your daily minimum. Can you envision a routine that takes under an hour? Or even thirty minutes? Remember that the point is that you can do it every day and that it doesn't take long. This is exactly how it should be. Make your daily minimum easy and appealing so it becomes a daily habit you enjoy.

5. **Make a "not to do" list.** What uses of your time are simply never good ones, even if you have abundant free time? Make note of them so that they are easy to spot and avoid engaging. And when you accidentally fall into a rabbit hole with them, review this list and make note of actions and pastimes you can replace the time-wasting habits with in your daily concentric-circles model.

6. **Engage your tomorrow self.** Next time you face some task that you really don't want to do right now, have a talk with your tomorrow self. Ask: *What do you want to be doing?* Maybe it is this very thing, with more time and leisure. Or maybe it is something else entirely, in which case you'll see the real reason why it's best to do today's task today. By respecting the time and wishes of your tomorrow self—and by realizing that this self will almost certainly be there tomorrow

feeling either annoyed or grateful for the actions of your today self—you'll feel less likely to hedge and procrastinate.

7. **Make the uncomfortable comfortable.** Choose one thing that you feel the need to do (but really don't want to or are having trouble getting started on!). Think of a few slight ways you can change it so that you enjoy it more. How can you invest it with some pleasure or more immediate incentive? This can also be reversed for great effect in the realm of growth and courage. Try making something that is currently too comfortable into a slight challenge.

8

ACCEPT THE EXCEPTIONS

Leaving Margins and Keeping Perspective

Voluntary change is one thing. But what about involuntary change? Times when the world shifts without your planning for it to—often suddenly, sometimes beautifully, sometimes terribly, and always leaving tracks?

There are both happy and sad days that change everything, that create in our lives a sort of before-and-after. These are the exceptions—we remember them in almost cinematic clarity among the years of ordinary days that we will likely remember in a hazier, more general way. Often when people look back on unhappy exceptions—surviving great suffering or hardship—they speak of both the compassion and the clarity that come with the act of accepting the irreparable loss and sifting through the ashes to create a new life. The same clarity may come too, with happy exceptions. Recently, a friend felt guilty for being unavailable in the weeks after falling suddenly in love. *I will see you when I'm back in real life again*, she wrote. Part of my work as her friend was to tell her to perish the guilt by way of reminding her that this is her real life too, just an exceptional part of it. We must accept that in exceptions, we may drop everything else for a spell.

Whatever the exception is—a happy one or a hard one that leaves us reeling—there are a few ways to cultivate a mindset of compassion, resilience, gratitude, self-trust, and willingness to see the world as it is, coupled with a nimble readiness to pivot fast, to tilt without capsizing, and to find perspective.

STUDY HISTORY TO FIND PERSPECTIVE

A valuable way to see our lives through a lens of our good fortune, even on challenging days, is to step back and get perspective. Ask: How does your life look when seen alongside other lives throughout time? Traveling brings perspective because we see both how other people live now and how they have lived in earlier ages. (Go to any castle. The beds of kings are less comfortable than yours.)

Whenever I find myself seeing things only from my own small perspective, feeling that something is a crisis that perhaps isn't, or seeing something as impossible that I will almost certainly live through, or seeing something as higher stakes than it really is, or thinking I have more control than I really do—it helps me to think about our ancestors.

None of our ancestors expected the comforts that we take for granted today. They lived more simply (though not, I think, nearly as comfortably). Their ancestors lived more simply still. Socrates lived more simply. Jane Austen. Galileo. Laura Ingalls Wilder. Shakespeare—and he lived through the plague, though his son died of it. Think of every person who contributed something important to the world as you know it. Did they not live through harder things than we are living through? What did they have in abundance? What did they not have at all?

Humans are resourceful, built to survive—until we're not. Like any animal body, our bodies know things beyond our daily control, even if we try mightily to control them. We must keep the perspective that we do not need to take so seriously our everyday tasks, needs, and responsibilities. We are not Atlas and the world does not belong on our shoulders. If we rest, it is unlikely that our world will fall apart.

One of my greatest eureka moments involving perspective at home happened in the grocery store. I was doing a late-night run for diapers and oatmeal when one of the employees asked how I was doing. I answered honestly, a ranty grumble about messy kitchens and people not helping out. I had told her the truth, and she could have dismissed it and gone back to her work, or just laughed in commiseration. But instead, she stopped me in my tracks by offering a perspective from outside myself. She said:

"One day your house will be spotless. Your kids will have grown and you may have outlived your spouse. But you will be all alone." I took this perspective home, cleaned the mess, and kissed all my people, feeling urgently aware and appreciative of this finite era of having them in my house. Even years later, if I feel tempted to grumble about the life I live and love, I remember this kind stranger's words. Keeping perspective helps us see what we have (a houseful of loved ones)—and not dwell so much on what we don't (an effortlessly spotless kitchen). It helps us see the bigger picture.

There is a Stoic principle called negative visualization, in which you imagine all the things in your life gone, so that even their challenges feel like something to be appreciated as they are. That is what this stranger was helping me do: envision what my days would be without these beautiful complications that were and are, in fact, my life.

To me it feels like the opposite of positive thinking, which is equally useful. While positive or hopeful thinking envisions our best-case realistic life scenarios (everyone at home learns to cooperate and keep a clean house so we can all enjoy each other!), negative visualization offers the worst-case realistic scenario—what life would look like if everything we had were gone (no house, no family, no love, no dishes, no food). As starkly different as they are, these two modes of imagining can help us see the range of what is possible in our lives as they are.

It is worth trying to engage in both thought exercises each time you need to reframe something. They help us prepare for both the best and the worst, and to enjoy the present in between. They help us turn our attention toward engaging in our lives wholeheartedly, and away from what we cannot control (the world news, our children's futures) and what might not be worth wasting our energy on constantly trying to control (our partner's habit of leaving socks on the bathroom floor). It is a simple exercise in feeling grateful for the abundance of what we have—maximizing what is positive in our lives—and shedding our annoyance at things that don't ultimately matter—minimizing what is negative.

I count among my close friends a surprising number of centenarians, people alive and flourishing at age one hundred. When I was writing a biography of my grandfather, who lived to age 103, I started researching what science has to say about centenarians. I became obsessed (I bet that if you started reading about them, you'd become obsessed too—it is well worth a deep dive). In addition to the elements frequently studied by scientists—how centenarians eat, exercise, and socialize—noteworthy also is the simplicity of their lives and their ability to keep perspective: to keep calm and carry on, no matter what life throws their way.

Studies of centenarian hot spots—referred to by some scientists as "blue zones"—show that the world's longest-lived people live in smaller, humbler dwellings than Americans today expect to inhabit; they rely to some extent on modern medicine to stay healthy, but primarily on common sense, whole foods, ample time with friends, a low-stress life, and daily exercise. They do a lot of work by hand that we outsource to machines (such as kneading one's own bread or sweeping the floor). As they age, they are not moved into nursing homes, but kept at the heart of a multigenerational family where they help with the labor of the home: cooking, housework, childcare, and other physical and mental tasks. In short, centenarians tend to live simple, well-edited, physically active lives, with people and community at the center.

This is, in fact, how people have lived for millennia. The communities with the highest percentage of long-lived people simply have these daily healthy acts built into their culture. These people were born before airplanes, disposable diapers, and robot vacuums. By today's standards, they have lived humble lives in their comfort and wants—but lives of terrific bounty in terms of their needs. Indeed, this population is exemplary in terms of keeping perspective—seeing the good in their lives and feeling their own purpose, while accepting the difficulty of doing what must be done.

My grandfather was one of these. He maintained thousands of good friendships, calling his former students on their birthdays; he used his body as a machine rather than outsourcing physical labor onto other people or other machines until he was well into his eighties: pushing stalled cars, mowing his own lawn, climbing onto the roof to unclog a drain. My dad recalls a story when, after a hernia surgery, my grandfather was told by his doctor not to drive, advice he followed. But when a stranger's car stalled, my grandfather raced out of the restaurant to push it!

Thinking about lives like these inspires and humbles me—I live such a 2D life in contrast! But it helps me see the options I have and how I might work with them. If I can try a simpler way, I should. If I can say one kind thing before making a correction or a request, I should. If I can bring dinner to an ailing friend, rather than just sticking my head back into the dirt of my day, I might as well. If I can be the machine rather than having a machine— walking instead of driving, for example, or visiting a neighbor instead of texting her—I will. If I can lighten even one of my dependencies, I should. If I can be less acquisitive, more generous, I will. If I can see "we" before "me," this experiment in editing will have been a success.

And when all else fails, if you are looking round your life—as we all do—and having *a day* and forgetting all perspective and knowing that another round of learning an old familiar lesson is around the corner, stop what you are doing and find someone young to observe. For, as author Rachel Clarke observed in her memoir, "No one is able to inhabit the present quite like those aces of nowness, our children." What we have is today, and very likely, tomorrow. And this is something.

What we have is today.

BE PORTABLE

To journey well, we must travel lightly. I heard a teacher say: "We come to the world empty-handed and we leave it empty-handed;

so we have nothing to worry about, nothing to lose, nothing to fear." Another friend says, to the same effect: "Life is a series of wombs." Before we are born, our food and our home exist in a single person: our mother. We live there until we are too heavy to carry, and then we exit that womb and move into another—then another—and then the final womb is death. In both of these quotes, the same point holds: We cannot ever stay in one place, holding the same things, even if we wanted to. Portability is bred into us.

Portability comes from the Latin word that means "to carry"; it means the quality of being light or small enough to be easily moved. Portability matters, not only through place, in terms of travel across geography, but also through time, in terms of travel through life's eras and seasons.

To live an edited life is to be prepared for exceptional times— times when you must go all in to meet a deadline, or when you fall in or out of love, or realize that a person or a situation needs you now, and you must throw everything else aside. An exception is when we must deal with new information, whether a job promotion or a scary diagnosis. Whether for better or worse, we must change tactics.

Often the exceptions are a shock to our system: they suggest that an era is ending, and remind us that one day we will end. There is nothing like awareness of our mortality to help us see the big picture. The good old memento mori idea that a reminder of death is a catalyst for living fully and in respect of life's

Make editing a life practice.

shortness. Living portably reminds us to edit now. Do not wait until death, wealth, or until you have more time. Edit now. Edit always. Make editing a life practice.

It takes a lot of drafts to get something as distilled and effective as it can be. A packing list. A poem. A daily routine. A relationship. Your first aid kit. If you return at intervals to look at it critically and carefully, all the excess and much of the indecision get eventually honed away.

An edited life is portable by nature. By practicing being portable, we take pleasure in our lives while we are living them, and we let go easily when we must let go. This form of nonattachment is always life's most essential wisdom—easy to say, but a lifetime's worth of work to practice.

RETHINK THE SCAFFOLDING

When we face an exception, we learn fast that a great deal of our life, even in its edited form, we had built as scaffolding in case the whole structure falls down. A reservist spouse is called to active duty; a child leaves for college; a beloved dog must be put down. The structure around these relationships—the weekly dates with the spouse, the active parenting of a child living at home, the daily trips to the dog park—is no longer needed. What it once held up is gone or has changed.

This correlates with something I know of editing: sometimes you need a scaffolding to find the right shape, but then when you're ready, you can let it go.

Like bay leaves in a soup, they were there for flavoring. Not for themselves.

I learned this lesson in another way when I accepted the immense job of writing a biography of my grandfather, a coal miner turned chemical engineer. This task fell to me at an exceptional time—when I began the writing process, I had a newborn. And even without a newborn and the general lack of time and sleep and clarity of thought, I was a poet and not a biographer. I had no idea how to do it.

The genre of biography felt heavy, like it would teeter and collapse the moment I tried to raise it—also, I had no real understanding of the science at the heart of his life's work. But one day I realized that his life story echoed a well-known fairy tale: "Jack and the Beanstalk." It was about a boy who climbed out of the mines, facing a few giants along the way, to bring riches and hope to his family and community. So I set myself a finite research period, and afterward I simply wrote his life as I knew it, fitting in the science I knew and adding the shorthand XX for what would need to be filled in eventually. In between each chapter, I wrote a lyrical retelling of Jack and the giant. It was fun! I found as I went along that I loved writing his life from birth to age one hundred, calling him weekly for questions that only he'd be able to answer, and braiding in the fairy tale. I finished a draft (by this time my new-born was a toddler), then hired a research assistant to help me get all the science right. I showed the finished book proudly to my writing mentor. "Well done," she said. "Now you can take out all the fairy tales."

I balked at first. I loved the fairy tales—they made it possible for the book to be written! But my target audience was made up of chemical engineers—my grandfather's students—and they want-ed to read about him, not about beans and giants. My scaffolding had enabled me to raise the book to what it needed to be. I removed the fairy tales—and the book still held.

A physical analogy would be a weak ligament. You wear a brace and strengthen the muscles around it so that you can still use that joint.

And so with your life. What scaffoldings bear the weight of your life's structures? What would you do if outside forces made it so that scaffolding fell apart? Explore the ways in which the habits of your life—its musculature, so to speak—uphold what matters to you. Are any old scaffoldings needing to be taken down? Do any current scaffoldings bear too much weight?

Reconsidering our scaffolding allows us to create new scaffold-ings as needed to support new eras. Currently, I have a personal scaf-folding to mark the seasons. Like any personal practice, it is very specific to my own needs. It is a way to look over the season that has ended and adjust my life for the coming season and whatever surprises it may carry. Your seasonal routine may involve gardening, grandchildren, volunteering, camping trips, or travel. Here is mine:

- Read from Cheering Section (a document where I keep encouraging words from loved ones).

- Swap out closet for season.

- Refresh to-do list for the season (triage it: either complete tasks or jettison).

- Touch base with a few dear friends whom I haven't seen in the last season.

- Set appointments for personal care and health.

- Make sure each kid has some form of sport and art to practice.

- Plan a few seasonal family adventures and put them on the calendar.

- Glance over the past three months of my calendar—just to notice what's there.

We will always have scaffolding for our lives—it is a form of daily minimum for our months and years—and it is well worth it to examine whether the scaffolding is as strong as we need it to be, and whether any of it needs to be periodically rebuilt, and whether it is holding up the things that we still want held up.

Sometimes, in exceptional seasons, the scaffolding is all we have, and we will cling to it like a lifeboat: it will be the thing that keeps us afloat. Other times, we find that we can float well enough without it, and we can release some of the scaffolding and simply face our lives.

TILT WITHOUT CAPSIZING

Sometimes we tilt one way or the other. In a sailboat, the correct way to tilt without capsizing is to depower the sail. Wind knocks you over, so close that you can see your reflection in the water. Slow down and the boat stabilizes, then you start over, slowly. This requires lightness and agility and a good hand on the ropes.

If we do not correct it, tilting becomes a problem. One day or one week without exercise is no real crisis. A year is. A day of neglecting some part of life, we will survive. A week of neglect may take some time to fix, but we can probably fix it. Much longer than that, if we tilt away from what matters most, there are real consequences. We can apologize, repair . . . but everyone feels better if we don't capsize.

This week I've been working extra hours. Next week I will pause and stabilize the balance. I will be available more for my people. We must be able to distinguish what must happen today and what can happen another time. We must know what is essential and what can be released. And we also must get creative.

When James and I became parents—knowing full well that we'd undoubtedly have a few major capsizes—we made a panic-button arrangement. If either one of us felt 70 percent overwhelmed as the on-duty parent, we'd call the other immediately and say, "Help!" Then we'd swap duty. We never abused this privilege, but we both did use it to avoid capsizing—I'd estimate no more than half a dozen times each. Sometimes it meant having to cancel something work related or really, really fun in order to run home to the baby and the stressed-out spouse. But when you think about how much collateral damage comes from being 100 percent overwhelmed, it is well worth it to pause before hitting that particular guardrail and let someone else shoulder the day's burden, giving the overwhelmed person time to reset.

We also have a family signal when we are somewhere together and one person is ready to leave. We call it "the elephant," and it is a slight waving of one arm to look like a trunk. It is not at all subtle, and we respect it entirely. James and I developed this signal after being accidentally left at a wedding at the San Francisco Zoo, when both of our rides left without us. We might've stayed there all night among the elephants if the bride's mom hadn't made a special trip back to collect more gifts and found us. So ever since then, we've used this gesture to avoid getting stuck. Always if one person is ready to go, and we're in the same car, we leave "at first elephant." Now the kids are old enough to use this system too. We leave before we falter. We leave before we lose our charm.

No day will go exactly the way we plan it—and some will tilt further than others from what we feel to be the right balance. The next time you feel yourself tilting more than you'd like to, try out some form of this idea. Pause. Slow down. Depower the situation by assessing how tilted it really is and trying to get a clear perspective on what you need to do next. Then correct your balance as soon as you are ready.

There will always be wind pushing us this way and that—both surprises and anticipated challenges coming our way. Build into your life some agreements or signals with the people you love that allow you easily to do this. If we can depower a situation and tilt together to avoid a capsize, then we all stay on the boat.

ALLOW SPACIOUS MARGINS

We are never, ever perfect. Nor are we ever done editing. Therefore, part of a well-edited life means leaving margin for error, for growth, and for anything else that arises.

In a life without margins, we spend a lot of time trying to be perfect. When we are strapped for time, we have to count minutes exactly; when we are strapped for money, we have to count dollars exactly. But if we leave ample margins, and if we are kind and reasonable and live a well-edited life as a general practice, we stay well buffered on the days when we fall off the boat.

Only then we can relax and do our best without fear.

Margins are a form of making the day elastic: plan it out halfway, leave open the other half to what will come. Ideally, both at work and at leisure, we should leave a few hours each day open. In a month, we might leave a few open days. In a year, it is well worth leaving certain weeks strategically blank. Margins in a day are like the extra holes on your belt: when you eat sensibly you don't need them, but every once in a while . . . you're glad to have them! When we are perfect, and when those around us are perfect, we do not need it. But generally, we are not perfect, so this model allows forgiveness, elasticity, and ease.

Time margins are a special challenge for me: I love to fill my day to the very top, and I sometimes do this, but I recognize that at times it can leave me racing around and not fully enjoying any of the activities I've chosen. I continue to do it because I find that if my day is full, I'm more likely to do one thing, then another, without procrastinating any of them—simply because I want to have time to do the next thing.

The daily minimum makes this possible. We've done our vital things already, so the rest of the day can come at us, like a beautiful wild beast, and we'll have the ability to track it or at least make way. If everything goes wrong at 10:00 a.m., at least by breakfast I've moved forward in the two or three places that matter. Well-triaged days with margins mean that you can work hard first thing and relax in the afternoons and evenings, and that ideally you can be ahead of your schedule, and not behind.

Margins are excellently helpful to think about in our financial life. What do you need to leave in savings, untouched—just in case? Can you put some percentage of your earnings directly into a savings account and think of the rest as what you can spend? Then during months of big spending, expensive repairs, or splurge vacations, you can tilt without capsizing because you have left such spacious margins.

We will never be airtight from bad things happening, but we can do our best to control what we can and not spend our days in worry. If we plan our lives without margins, we will never feel the pleasure of wandering into happy chaos, into the promising unmapped future. If we try to control everything, we will never allow ourselves to be changed by the wisdom of facing exceptions with humility, curiosity, and grace. When you edit your life, you think about your life's true shape. In simple increments, you bend the real to meet the ideal. The margins are the places for surprise, spontaneity, and growth.

80 PERCENT IS GOOD ENOUGH

By the time you've gotten here in this book, you've done the work and built the guardrails. Hooray! This is worth celebrating. Of course you will get derailed sometimes, and that's okay, for you have the skills to clean it up. My friend, a former professional athlete, says: "Sometimes the master must break the rules she's set for herself."

Sometimes we are tempted to perfect something before we even begin. The areas where I am most susceptible to perfectionism are in time management and healthy eating. The early tips I learned about being organized regarding time helped me hugely—but now improving my time management is not the best use of my time. And in the healthy-eating realm, I spent a decade reading books about food science and nutrition, visiting naturopaths and asking detailed questions so I could learn from my doctors. Then finally one day I realized: I know enough. Actually, I didn't realize it. A nutritionist friend, whom I was grilling about cruciferous vegetables, placed her hand on my arm and gently said, "You know, all of your worry about eating well is worse for you than just being imperfect." Point taken.

Laura Vanderkam, time management expert, wisely notes that sometimes we must "maximize" something (give it our best and then some), and other times we can afford to "satisfice" it (let good enough be good enough). There are points in all of our lives that we can stop trying to turn into holy grails and simply let be.

When our system falls apart (or when *we* fall apart) for a week or for a month, no problem—as long as 80 percent of the time, we honor our guardrails, then we can clean up the mess and get back to good. The wisdom to let 80 percent be good enough is fundamental to enjoying the journey, trusting oneself and one's people, owning our days and our lives—however lopsided and imperfect.

For life is full of chaos: handfuls of blueberries sent through the laundry, arguments, illness, months we come up short when bills are due. We must expect these things. We must budget our time, money, and energy—daily, yearly, monthly—to afford to be a little fuzzy on a day-to-day basis. Eighty percent is just fine. It helps us accept our humanity.

With housework, 80 percent has to be perfect, especially when living with children, pets, or messy housemates. "Have you done your sweeping with your whole heart?" My husband asks this of our son. "Yes," my son says, straight-faced and holding the broom, surrounded by a thousand pieces of confetti and a stepped-on banana skin. Because we are only 80 percent perfect, we do not have a response ready—but this leaves room for his sister to step in before we can, gently asking: "Can I help you look one more time?"

Putting aside 20 percent in any aspect of life requires that we trust—ourselves, our families, our bodies, our community. Striving for perfection is an act born from fear, not from love—and certainly not from self-trust. It may feel impossible to eat perfectly vegetarian, but what if we aimed to be an "imperfect vegetarian" and eat that way 80 percent of the time? That would probably feel easy and satisfying. You could also be an "imperfect early riser," "imperfect meditator," "imperfect bedtime story reader," or an "imperfect teetotaler." There are many options. It may feel that any one of the systems in this book is all fine and good, but who can do it all the time? Don't worry about that. Try it for 80 percent of the time in a single week, or day, or in the next hour. Make the margins whatever you need in order to feel safe and content and hopeful.

The final word on this: Don't over-worry your life. Trust that hitting the mark 80 percent of the time is an excellent place to aim. It is—this is both a benefit and a goal of a good life-edit. You are free to worry less. You can see your life clearly, both in good times and bad, and can love it as it is.

LIFE-EDIT PROMPTS

1. **Try negative/positive visualization.** Next time you feel annoyed at or afraid of something, do a thought experiment of taking this hiccup to its far positive and negative extremes. Say your plane is late. In the positive, this might give you time for an in-depth conversation with a stranger, who ends up offering you a fabulous work opportunity and introducing you to his daughter, who ends up becoming the *best* best friend you've ever had. In the negative, you might miss your work meeting and get fired and then run out of money and have to sell your house, in which case your spouse would get fed up and leave. The reality of our lives is usually between these two extremes—one is the fantasy and the other is the opposite of a fantasy (maybe we could call it *antasy*?), but thinking of both in rich detail can offer a useful perspective.

2. **Remove something from your worry bank.** Are there any points where you are over-worrying your life— where things are good enough and you are meddling

with them by trying to holy-grail them? I am susceptible to trying to make my calendar perfect—which, of course, takes valuable time away from the things that are supposed to go onto my calendar! What do you over-worry or (perhaps unnecessarily) try to holy-grail? Perhaps it is something that you think a lot about but that is not a big deal to just *do*. Or perhaps you are trying to control something—or someone—that cannot be controlled. Write down any parts of your life that do not belong in your worry bank or that are fine enough as they are.

3. **Consider your surrenders.** What in your life could you surrender? Do you fight some part of your body every day (such as your hair)? Can you let it do its natural thing? Are there moments in the past where you have surrendered trying to control something and been better for it? Look back over the years and try to identify these moments—so that future surrenders can be seen as portals to new forms of lightness and ease.

4. **Shed the scaffolding.** Look around your life and identify the scaffolding. Perhaps it is an object: a bin of clothes for a career you started but chose not to pursue. By giving away the suits, you shed both clothes you do not need and the needless clinging to a life avenue that you will never, as far as you now know, need to take. What

emotional scaffoldings or fear-based habits might you shed? Do you laugh nervously because you are afraid of listening well? Do you say yes too quickly out of fear of offending? Look around for scaffolding habits—ask yourself: *Can my life hold without them?*

5. **Discuss margins aloud.** Consider where you might expand margins in your life: financial, time-wise, sleep-wise, anything you can think of. Brainstorm with a friend or a family member about what these margins might be. Devise signals or reminders or guardrails that you can use to remember to respect them.

6. **List practice vs. perfect.** Make a list of things you do in an ordinary month: Which are practices and which need to be perfect? A meal does not have to be perfect—unless you are serving it to the queen. A tennis match with a friend—not perfect—though you would strive for perfection in a big match. A work deliverable might need to be perfect, or not, depending. Are there any places you are striving for perfection where 80 percent would work just as well?

Farewell

Well, here you are.

These skills for life-editing are yours now. You have thought about the shape your life might take. In simple increments, you have bent the real to meet the ideal. You have left margins for spontaneity, self-correction, growth, and surprise. You have the ability to edit your life—any part of your life at any time.

With these skills you have practiced and the knowledge you have gained, you can trust yourself to enjoy your days. You can, at any time you choose, tend your first choices and daily minimums. You can add to the green. You can see your life clearly from season to season, and you can love it as it is.

This is a good time to list out the souvenirs that you wish to take forward, upon closing this book and rising to face your life. What do you need less of than you thought? What do you need more of? What would feel good to make part of your daily minimum—and what would feel good to shed? Which two or three life-edits do you need the most urgently right now? Which ones do you find intriguing but less urgent—that you wish to lay away for a rainy day? Is there someone with whom you wish to share your ongoing life-editing journey?

In reading this, you know how to shed. You know that everything is a choice, be it having breakfast with someone you love, or going into the cold dark morning to do your work, alone, until hunger sets in. All of these are valid choices. Life has enough room for each one to exist, to repeat itself in a long bead necklace of time, to be remembered.

You know too, by now, that your time, energy, and attention are your most valuable resources—and in living an edited life, you are valuing those resources as much as they deserve, and stewarding them well. In living in such a way, your life—in ways, perhaps, you do not even know—will inspire others along their own journeys.

You can't rewind time. But you can live life in distinct, well-edited seasons that give you the chance to enjoy the best green your days have to offer, and to add a little to the world's green as well. There will be eras in your life for big sweeping edits, grand gestures for all the world to see—and eras for tiny near-invisible edits, personal ones that nobody sees but you.

When we made the single edit of moving to the Shed, we had no idea what would come of it. It was a single edit—yet it changed our whole life for the better. If all you can edit today is your weekend schedule or your sock drawer, do it. Give yourself that gift. Trust that a small edit today will make it easier to edit the next thing tomorrow. Indeed, tomorrow's edit might happen organically without your even trying.

Because editing begets editing.

Editing begets editing.

Big house or small house; town or country; hosting or guesting; or any life you live, you have given yourself the editing habit, and it will not easily go away.

For good habits are simple things, focusing our needs and wants in a single direction: Here. Now.

To be here now, to do the best we can do for our lives today, and for our world today. To enjoy the life we have, accept its limitations, and try not to waste it. To trust that we have edited our life to what it needs to be for now, and all that's left for us to do now is live in it.

As I write these final words, I hear my people waking up.

They will come into the main room and toast bagels for breakfast. My daughter will spread cardboard out on the table; she will put her breakfast neatly beside it and spend an hour deep at work making a school for her dolls, and I will notice—and try not to say—how much her school looks like the Shed. My son will point to the turquoise soccer ball when I emerge and I will follow him outside for a few kicks back and forth in the cold morning. Soon afterward, James will wake and put on music and do a dorky-dad dance and the kids will giggle maniacally and, depending on their moods, join him. I will tell them that I just finished writing a book with all of us in it and that they can choose their names.

"Cora," Cora will say after a moment of thought, then she will return to her cardboard.

"Booger!" Scott will yell, looking around to see if he's made his sister laugh. She will laugh—he will be satisfied—then she will shake her head and say he needs to think of something not so embarrassing.

We will spend most of the day in the same room. If this day is like other days, we will laugh and talk about things great and small. If it is like other days, it will contain both joys and challenges. We will add this day to a growing stack of days that, we hope, we will look back on and remember with joy.

I don't know if this is happily ever after but it's happily right now. And I wonder if happily ever after isn't simply a series of well-edited days of happily right now stacked together.

I wish you a lifetime of happily right now.

Thanks

Thanks to Sascha and Larry, this book's soul guides; to the team at TarcherPerigee, a first-choice team of editors, and especially to the warm, brilliant Marian Lizzi; to Nancy, my writing fairy godmother; and to Josh, who keeps us fed and sung to; to Lynn, always, who taught me to love editing; to my inspiring parents and parents-in-law, for being lovingly supportive of our many life-edits (once the initial horror wears off!); to all my friends who asked the right questions to help me find my own way; to Kim Cross, whose writing life stands as one of my worthiest models; to Allison, Cat, Eliza, Heather, Jenn, Kel, Laura, Marney, Talaya, Tamrah, Yo-El, and Mom—beta readers extraordinaire; to Laura Vanderkam, whose books have been my continuing ed for adulthood; to the Vixens, who add to the green in countless ways; to all of my beloved students, whose questions and ideas have enriched my days; to everyone at the café and the hotel (you know who you are!) where I wrote so much of this book; to all the creative thinkers and minimalists before me whose writings have taught us all to look anew—literally to revise—our lives; and to James, my best friend through so many seasons, who makes all things possible.

About the Author

Elisabeth Sharp McKetta is an award-winning author, teacher, and speaker. She is the author of ten previous books including the writing guide *The Creative Year* and the novel *She Never Told Me About the Ocean*. Her shorter writings have appeared in *Real Simple*, *The Poetry Review*, *Mid-American Review*, *Literary Mama*, and elsewhere. She teaches writing for both Oxford Department of Continuing Education and Harvard Extension School, where she won the James E. Conway Excellence in Teaching Writing Award. She also leads workshops to help businesses and individuals tell their stories and organize their missions. Her TEDx talk "Edit Your Life like a Poem"—the inspiration for this book—offers a framework for editing a life to its best version, based on her experience living with her family for three years in a tiny backyard guesthouse at the base of the Rocky Mountain foothills so they could all focus more on what matters. You can find her at elisabethsharpmcketta.com.